PASTORAL ADMINISTRATION

PASTORAL ADMINISTRATION

by

ARTHUR MERRIHEW ADAMS

Philadelphia
THE WESTMINSTER PRESS

LIBRARY OF CONGRESS CATALOG CARD NO. 64–18686

PUBLISHED BY THE WESTMINSTER PRESS®

PHILADELPHIA, PENNSYLVANIA

PRINTED IN THE UNITED STATES OF AMERICA

Contents

Preface

This book is for pastors and persons preparing to be pastors. It should also be of use to church officers. Through the use of the table of contents and index one may go straight to things that are of immediate interest.

Part One, " Principles and Practices," sets forth a viewpoint on administration, then deals with the pastor's disciplined use of his own time. The chapters that follow develop the major categories of administration: planning, organization, personnel, and leadership. No denominational stance is assumed. " Official board " is used as a generic term for the authoritative group in the local congregation, which may have such designations as session, vestry, or consistory.

Part Two, " Program," deals with a multitude of possibilities in chapters on worship, nurture, witness, and supporting activities. It is intended as a reference section. Part Three, " Power," consists of one chapter on " Success and Failure." An annotated bibliography is provided for the convenience of those who wish to pursue subjects further. The author obviously owes much to the books that are listed, though the format of this volume is different from any other in the field of church administration.

The orientation is practical. The major purpose will be served if pastoral administration is improved at the local level. However, the arrangement highlights a number of subjects that cry out for further theological reflection or careful research. One may hope that this will give rise to a ferment of experimentation and thought, and to books on other aspects of church administration. It is possible also that scholars with limited pastoral experience may welcome this cross section of American church life as they prepare to engage in discussions on the nature of the ministry and the structure of the congregation.

I have been aware as I have written that I am much in debt to the people of the four congregations I have served in the last thirty years. The Seaside Park Union Church, a two-year student charge, on the New Jersey coast was the community center for a village of perhaps two hundred souls, which expanded in the summer for vacationists. Glading Memorial Presbyterian Church, in northeast Philadelphia, asked the presbytery to ordain and install me the night it was organized. It ministered during the depression of the thirties to industrial folk who were reduced to paying rent for homes they once owned. Then it grew rapidly with the new prosperity and the endless extension of row houses. The ancient First Presbyterian Church of Albany stands on capitol hill, and the Central Presbyterian Church of Rochester, New York, is at the heart of that remarkable city. These two congregations have made creative responses to their downtown opportunities and problems. They were well equipped to educate their pastor. Businessmen and industrialists in these churches introduced me to management principles, taught me the use of a budget in the projection and control of a program, made priceless suggestions about leadership and personnel practices, and proved the importance of having as church officers some men used to taking risks!

It is not possible even to list the names of all who had a part in one pastor's education in administration. Staff associates, by their suggestions and questions, encouraged experiments and thought about what was going on. Ministers and elders have come to discuss problems in a wide variety of churches during the years I have served presbyteries as ministerial relations chairman. J. Keith Louden, Vice-President of the American Management Association, and a long-time associate on the Board of Trustees at Princeton Theological Seminary, has graciously opened to me the research facilities of the AMA and was my host at a briefing for top management sponsored by the Presidents' Association at the AMA Grove in Hamilton, New York. He has also given generously of his time for the courses on church administration we have offered together at Princeton Seminary's Center of Continuing Education. My colleagues in the faculty at the seminary, while in no way responsible for what I have written, have thrown light on a number of subjects in discussion. Thanks are also due my secretary, Mrs. Madeline M. Simpson. Without her editorial help and work on the manuscript the book could not have come into being. Margaret Adams, my wife, daughter of a minister-editor and mother of a minister, made invaluable suggestions and also prepared the index.

A. M. A.

Princeton, New Jersey

PART ONE

PRINCIPLES AND PRACTICES

CHAPTER I

Thinking About Administration

God was ready to do great things for his people in Egypt, but he needed Moses. Centuries later Samuel was struggling to maintain the illusion that no earthly organization or administration was necessary; let the people merely hear the Word of God through the prophet. He has sons today!

It is obvious to any reader of the New Testament that the hungry and fractious sheep of the first generation required more of the apostles than preaching and individual interest. These things were important, but so were the administrative tasks involved in councils, deputations, special offerings, elections, training plans, and missionary journeys. The same fact leaps at you from the pages of Christian history, whether you are reading of Ignatius in the first century, Irenaeus in the second, Cyprian in the third, Ambrose in the fourth, Augustine or Patrick in the fifth; whether you are thinking of Boniface or Bernard, Luther or Calvin, Wesley or Carey. In every generation the people of God need administrators, men of words and actions, and some are called to this task. It is essentially the pastoral task: to lead the flock, not as of right, but as humble instruments of Christ the Good Shepherd.

Administration is working with and through people to get things done. The English word developed from the Latin verb meaning "to serve." The major Biblical word is a term that means "servant" or "waiter." It is most often translated "minister" and has come into our language as "deacon." Jesus uses the term when he says, "The Son of man came not to be ministered unto, but to minister." It appears in the sense of "administer" in Paul's letters.

It is interesting that in all three languages the person designated to serve others ended up as the one they chose to help them get things done. Certainly, "administer" now has a clearly "executive" or "managerial" intent. The administrator must plan, organize, find and train leaders and workers, offer some guidance, and encourage discipline. This is true whether the people to whom he is related are engaged in playing a game, earning a living, fighting a war, attacking a social evil, or responding to the divine love in worship, nurture, and witness. Someone must be engaged in administration if a group is to do anything together.

The church is a group of people. They have been drawn to Christ and to one another by the love of God revealed in the life and death and resurrection of Jesus Christ and by the life-giving power of the Spirit of God. He cleanses them continually and teaches them to know themselves as children of God, and encourages them to recognize all other men as their brothers. The fellowship of believers is under the administration of Christ, the great head of the church. He orders their lives, plans, organizes, finds and trains leaders and workers, offers guidance, and exercises discipline. But this is not done through new incarnations or by theophanies. The church is his body and is expected to carry out his purposes on earth.

The major purposes are related to his love and the responses it evokes; he lived and died to create a fellowship of love, living in communion with the Father, in mutual concern for one another, and in witness to the world. The church is a fellowship that exists for worship, mutual nurture, and witness. One person alone cannot do these things; they must be acts of the fellowship. The people must join together in worship and nurture and witness. Fortunately, Christ intends to lead them in these things.

He does so by placing his Word before the church in the Bible as it is read and preached. He does so by making the church relive his mighty acts of love in the Sacraments. He does so by pouring his life and love into the lives of his people so that there is an overflow.

But despite all this, something else must be done if his purposes are to be accomplished. To this end he raises up pastors. They are not to perform the ministry or service of the church;

only the whole church can do this. They are to do what must be done if the church is to perform its ministry, if all the people of God are to come together as a fellowship for worship and nurture and life in the world as witnesses. They are to do that from which the word "pastor" comes; they are to be shepherds under the great Shepherd. This is plainly an administrative task. It is more obvious when the New Testament uses the word "bishop," a synonym of "pastor," which also means "shepherd." It is equally clear when we recognize that the early pastors were usually "elders" in the old Hebrew tradition which expected leadership of those so designated.

The fellowship does not pass from an idea to a reality without human leadership. Attempts to carry the fellowship forward without some persons set aside for leadership have invariably resulted in the dissolution of that part of the fellowship or the gradual assumption of administrative responsibilities by someone. God's people must have someone who has time and special training to preach the Word, to administer the Sacraments, and to help them develop an order and shape for worship, using the best their fathers devised to respond to divine love and the choicest fruits of contemporary minds and hearts. God's people must have someone with time and training to marshal the gifts of the group as they seek to help one another wait upon God for growth in grace. There is in our day much talk of lay participation which ends in talk because there is not enough skilled administration. God's people must have someone with time and training to help them deploy effectively for witness in the world. One thinks of hundreds of people honoring Christ on their jobs, or working at tasks with slum children, with migrants, with prisoners, with the jobless, with retarded children, with gifted youth, and with diseased and hungry folk, and one knows that without a pastor whom Christ raised up none of this would have happened.

The administrative aspect of the pastor's task brings with it some temptations and dangers as do the other facets of his work. As a preacher, he is in jeopardy of posing and vain display, a love of the sound of his voice, an illusion that saying something is equivalent to doing it, a fatuous satisfaction with praise and interpretation of popularity as effectiveness, an exaltation of clever techniques at the expense of sincerity, and worst of all — the substitution of his own very human ideas for the gospel. As a visitor and counselor, he runs the risk of deteriorating into a salesman or an amateur psychiatrist, or even worse, into "playing God." As an administrator, the pastor is tempted to become more interested in programs than in people, to confuse institutional goals with divine purposes, to manipulate rather than lead, to forget that he is not a ruler but a servant and steward of his Lord. He is often enticed into substituting busywork with lists and files and office machines for the hidden hours of reading and prayer. The presence of temptation does not for a moment remove the necessity of performing the pastoral functions. The Lord himself was not deterred from his redemptive task by the necessity of risking temptation.

Each generation tends to highlight certain aspects of the pastoral task. H. Richard Niebuhr has documented this. Because in our time the common man has come into his own and is widely expected to take a vigorous, rather than a passive part in the life of the church, there is a new awareness of the importance of the administrative tasks that make wide participation possible. This development has a theological background that has been long in coming to focus. Paul's thrilling view of each Christian as a member of the body of Christ, designed and endowed for a special service to the whole body, has been more praised than taken seriously. The Biblical idea of the priesthood of all believers has been so long honored in the breach that men can, with straight faces, write books about the importance of participation in the life of the church by "the laity." The very emergence of these books, however, and of the vital activity of which they are echoes, is the fruit of a long work of the Holy Spirit.

In place after place large numbers of Christians are taking their calling seriously, and communicating the good news of God's love in Christ by word and deed in the midst of the world. They are meeting together and with non-Christians in small groups for Bible study and serious examination of implications of the gospel. They are expressing their faith at work and with fellow workers are exploring new ways of doing this. They are using vacation periods to learn how to be more effective Bible teachers or youth leaders. By the hundreds they are plunging out of comfortable suburbs to work in the inner city or in migrant camps. Untold numbers are offering themselves for Christian service overseas. Others are carrying the good news into the arts and music, or seeking to penetrate new frontiers of the mind for Christ, or struggling against social injustice.

The veriest fool can see that all this has its dangers. Christians may be overimpressed with the part they have in redemption. They may be tempted to forget the grace without which all their work is in vain. They may become so frantically busy that their lives lose the dimension of grace and the grace of love. The sheer size of the enterprise and the excitement of numbers may hypnotize them into a sort of fascination with process that is idolatry. All these dreadful things can happen, but they do not have to occur. In many places wide activity is a very healthy response of the whole people to the gospel. It is a refreshing change from the tired apathy of congregations sitting on their hands while leaders warn of activism and the world around them spins dizzily toward hell.

Something new and good is emerging in our time; a widespread participation of all the members in the action of the body, in its ministry to the world. This involves an increased emphasis on the administrative tasks of the pastor, which have always been a part of his calling. It is not necessary to use H. Richard Niebuhr's hyphenated word "pastor-director," for administrative leadership has always been a necessary part of the shepherd's task. It is to be expected of anyone called pastor.

It is still true, as Calvin wrote, that "wherever we see the Word of God purely preached and heard, and the sacraments administered according to Christ's institution, there it is not to be doubted, a Church of God exists." This places emphasis on two aspects of the pastor's task: preaching and conduct of Sacraments. But, note that even Calvin, reacting to abuses in the administrative functions of the pastoral office, nonetheless differentiates clearly between "pastors" and "teachers" who have concern "only with the interpretation of Scripture." Remember further that the Reformer, himself, spent much time in administration.

Long before the Reformation, the Head of the church said, "By this shall all men know that ye are my disciples, if ye have love one to another." This mark of the true church will appear wherever the Word is really *heard*. This wonderful love, revealed in the life and death of Jesus and pouring into our lives out of the life of Christ, makes us all want to do things for him and his. If we are to do them in an orderly and effective way, we must have pastors who are, among other things, administrators.

An important question remains. Can pastoral administration be done more efficiently? If this is possible, the people of God may be able, together, to do more for Christ or the pastor may have more time for his other tasks – or both of these desirable things may come to pass.

Robert Clyde Johnson tells us that "in a quite literal sense *every* administrative, procedural, and methodological question of the Church, however complex and involved its form may be, and however non-Biblical and nontheological it may appear at first glance, is in the last analysis reducible (and therefore should in the first analysis be reduced) to a single question: How would God have us serve here and now as his elect people, his chosen instrumentality, to communicate to the world his once-for-all reconciling act in Jesus Christ?" (*The Church and Its Changing Ministry,* edited by Robert Clyde Johnson, p. 106.) This sounds deceptively simple.

Let us suppose that the question confronting the church is, Who can be fed with the offering brought to Jerusalem by Paul? Several inquiries must be made and the final answer will be determined in part by subjection to disciplines far removed from Biblical hermeneutics, like arithmetic and business practice. Even questions of hermeneutics are answered to some degree through the secular disciplines of language study, archaeology, and history.

Again, let us put ourselves in the position of Boniface striding toward Germany in the name of Christ and confronted by a deep river. He will need the help of some very practical disciplines if he is to serve God according to his calling. The same thing is true of Robert Carey in India. Agricultural lore and the complicated knowledge of business and the printing art were essential. It was, moreover, answers found in physics and the acoustical science that enabled the American Bible Society to prepare for the evangelization of illiterate tribes by developing a remarkably effective, hand-operated record player.

This is true of administration. While its Biblical history goes back at least to Moses, it also has a long sequence of secular experience to be studied and construed. Materials may be gathered from spheres as diverse as the military, the political, and the industrial. The arts of the greatest practitioners may be copied and the modern science of administration, studied by hundreds of thousands, must be taken into account.

It is obvious that effort of this sort should increase the efficiency of pastoral administration. Certainly, other fields requiring administration have found rich rewards in studying the subject. The businessmen and industrialists of America, for example, spend vast sums for courses and books on administration. They use the resources of many universities and support the American Management Association, which has a multimillion dollar budget and conducts more than a thousand seminars a year. Clearly, this effort has had satisfactory results or it would not continue. Pastors should be able to increase their administrative efficiency by giving thoughtful attention to the subject.

The purpose of this book is to help in this process by examining pastoral activities in the light of the Word of God and the experience and thought of the church, and over against the categories and conclusions of secular research on administration.

Chapter II

The Pastor's Use of Time

The pastoral office inevitably involves a man in four activities: (1) personal relationships and ministries, (2) preaching and the conduct of worship, (3) teaching, and (4) administration. There are two other activities without which his ministry cannot be effective: (1) private devotions and (2) study.

Attempts to grade these things in order of importance or to make all the others tributary to one activity are as pointless as similar efforts in connection with heart, lungs, stomach, and liver. The fact that one activity takes longer than another, or is more noticed or appreciated, does not make it more important. Its value lies in its relation to the pastor's commission from his Lord.

1. Pastoral Priorities

a. Private devotional life has top priority in the sense that it has for all Christians. We are redeemed into communion with God, and the whole process of redemption loses point if it does not result in a close relationship with God. Jesus found time for prayer on the busiest days, and he prayed regularly for his friends. His servant can do no less.

The minister is fortunate beyond others in this respect because the needs of people around him join his own needs in driving him to a regular devotional life. The busier he becomes, the more he feels the need for prayer. Likewise, the heart-hunger of friends presses him to regular listening for God's Word in the Bible. The necessary relationships with fellow Christians in the church and with great souls met in biography and history lead the pastor to an ever-growing awareness of God, and a hunger for communion with him.

The pastor faces a temptation to turn his devotions into preparatory exercises for his other work. Devotional reading of Scripture and daily prayers enrich preaching and give depth to public prayers, but only so long as these are the by-products, not the purposes, of devotional hours. God will not be a means to an end. Persons who come to him making nice calculations debase the communion for which they were born. Those who come in love receive the ancient promise: they are blessed and become a blessing to others.

b. Personal relationships and ministries have top priority in the sense that when people have urgent needs everything else must wait. When someone is dying, the pastor does not bid him tarry until devotions are finished or a sermon is written. Like his Lord, the minister is primarily concerned about people.

Since he is serving a number of people, a plan is essential. The plan will be shaped by the pastor's theology. Since the church is called into being by the revelation of divine love, his major responsibility in dealing with persons is to make them aware of that love, and to help them find ways of expressing the love which springs up in them. The public reading and preaching of the Word have an important part in this, but if they do not continue personal conversations and result in personal conversations, they are likely to have little effect. The administration of the Sacraments has a part, but this, too, must occur in the context of a real fellowship in which pastor and people care for each other and share the common experiences of life.

Implications of this view include plans for: (1) the kind of mutual knowledge that arises as pastor and people worship and eat and work and play together, as did Jesus with his disciples, (2) the sharing of thought and feeling about God and the implications of his love in individual conversations and in small groups, (3) the readiness of the pastor to be on hand when, alone, a person may not be able to deal in a Christian way with a fine opportunity, a new adventure, a hard decision, a painful experience, a problem at home or on the job, an illness or bereavement. It will be noted that the first of these personal relationships and ministries occurs largely in connection with administration, the second with administration and pastoral care, the third with pastoral care alone – in the form of counseling and visitation and the conduct of funerals and weddings.

Pastoral care should have a high priority, but it must be the pastor's object constantly to reduce the number of situations in which persons cannot manage effectively alone. Our Lord, who was always responsive to human need, nonetheless sought to guide the growth of his disciples to the point where they could stand alone. Emergency needs will be fewer where the church life is planned to include a number of mutual experiences for pastor and people and where the pastor has come to know people in activities and groups as well as in their homes. Time spent on meetings and home visitation is often the most constructive from a pastoral viewpoint.

c. Preaching and the conduct of worship deserve high priority since the church does not exist without them. The proclamation of God's Word calls the church into being and sustains it, and acts of worship lie at the center of the church's life. The pastor is without excuse who neglects these things for other activities. Surveys indicate that most pastors spend a fifth to a quarter of their working hours in preparation for preaching and worship. This is probably adequate if there is one sermon a week, if the preparation time comes in uninterrupted mornings, if it is supplemented by generous provision for study and reading at other times, and if long summer periods are set aside for annual sermon planning and preliminary work on texts and outlines.

d. Teaching is one of the pastor's major functions, as it was crucial in his Lord's ministry. While studies show that the average minister devotes very few hours specifically to this task in any week, the teaching function may be exercised through most of the pastor's activities. Preaching and pastoral care and administration may be viewed as presenting opportunities for teaching.

Increasingly, ministers are planning their sermons with the obligation to teach in mind. Some meet with members of the congregation as they plan a sermon, and others invite questions and discussion of the sermon in a meeting following worship. In a number of cases preparatory Bible readings are suggested for the week before a sermon. Pastors are holding Bible classes at various hours with groups large and small. They are realizing that every meeting and action project is an opportunity to teach, if the minister is alert. They are seeing that a primary obligation is to instruct leaders of groups and the teachers of classes. They are recognizing that people learn by teaching others, so that the administrative task of involving folk in the enterprise of teaching may be the most effective way to instruct them. They are understanding the wisdom of our Lord, who expects all his people to be witnesses, knowing that in this way they will learn what they need to know about him, even as they reach others.

e. A pastor is, as we have seen, obligated to be an administrator. Other things must have priority over this aspect of his work, but this is merely a matter of orderly living; it should not suggest that administration is less important. It sets the context for the other activities. Adequate time must be set aside for it, or its necessities will intrude on other tasks and upset the most carefully devised time budget.

f. Every pastor intends to study in order that he may continue to grow. If this is to be done, it must be planned and subject to strict self-discipline. For most pastors study will share the morning hours with sermon preparation, and then be fitted into the time budget in other suitable places. Study time may be devoted to a mastery of books of the Bible, and make place for serious attention to theology, church history, and practical subjects. It will also make provision for some examination of developments in literature, art, and the sciences.

If this is to have cumulative value, there must be some pattern. During his summer sermon-planning days the pastor may outline his study plan for the year, coordinating Bible study and preaching projects. He may also arrange the sequence of subjects for study in such a way as to lay the fruits of this effort under tribute to the preaching. If a definite use is in sight for material, it is easier to achieve the discipline necessary for gathering it. Some pastors use other ways to take advantage of the human inclination to work harder on projects. They join or organize small study groups in which each member is under obligation to present a solid paper twice a year, and all agree to extensive reading. They write articles, which may be offered to theological journals or to religious or secular magazines of a popular character. They prepare reviews of current books for magazines or journals. They teach courses at nearby schools or seminaries.

An increasing number of pastors set aside a period in the late spring or early summer and another time in the fall for uninterrupted study, for the development of plans for study and preaching, and for building modest bibliographies for the year. Some churches are making this easier by providing two weeks of "sabbatical" time in each year. The seminaries are cooperating by the establishment of inexpensive residential centers and continuing education programs. Formal education is chosen by some pastors who find that they study more regularly under outside pressure. Many are close enough to a seminary or university to undertake graduate work one day a week. Very few who intend to remain pastors will find it advisable to resign a pastorate and devote full time to graduate study. There is great long-range value in the habits and skills that emerge as one makes study a part of the regular pastoral life.

Books that must be possessed for serious study and future reference should be purchased only after one has either read two good reviews or personally examined the book and compared it to others in the field. An annual visit to a good seminary library makes it possible to examine and compare a great many volumes, old and new, and opens the way to wiser purchases. Books may be borrowed directly or by mail from most seminary libraries. There is also a largely untapped resource in public libraries. Half of the pastors in this country make little or no use of the public libraries. An even larger number appear not to be aware that the public library can secure any book requested through the national interlibrary loan service. Use of this arrangement requires advance planning, but greatly enlarges the number of books available to the pastor.

General reading of novels, biographies, poetry, and plays will enrich a ministry as well as provide recreation, but this reading has no place in study time. One or two serious theological quarterlies may lend themselves to study and may help one develop a context for other study. Magazines, religious and secular, are important and some time must be found for them.

Like a good newspaper, which deserves twenty minutes a day, they have an important place in a pastor's life but must be fitted into periods set aside for general reading and recreation.

2. There Is a Time for Everything

It is probable that most ministers attempt to spend too much time on the job. The average pastor often works over ten hours a day. Recently a group of capable pastors tried, in vain, to reduce a practicable weekly time budget for a typical pastor to less than seventy-two hours.

Some of these hours are likely to be ineffectual. A group of company presidents at an American Management Association seminar so much enjoyed a day's management of an imaginary company that earned fantastic profits that they voted to continue the game after dinner in the evening, and proceeded to "lose" several million dollars. Midnight sessions with sermons, one more visit late in the evening, efforts at organizational tasks on days supposed to be free for rest, are often equally ineffective or even harmful to the minister's purposes, as well as to his long-term health and usefulness. But, what can be done about this?

Ecclesiastes reports out of reflection on long experience that there is a time for everything. The pastor will do well to think about this. The allocation of time must be related to several factors.

One is the ebb and flow of energy in each individual. Most men are at their best during the morning hours immediately after breakfast. Alertness usually drops off a bit after three hours and drifts down until lunch. This is accentuated if there is no change of pace. After a light lunch with some relaxation, the man is ready to go again, but concentration is not as easy as in the morning and energy flags sooner, though again a change of activity helps. After dinner there is a sluggish period, then several fairly energetic hours, which taper off as the evening wears on. A man can flog himself into high output over a fairly long period, but some fluctuation is inevitable and high-pressure efforts seem to follow a law of diminishing returns. Long-established habits, of course, affect the rate of energy output and alertness at any given time; family customs and physical makeup have something to do with this. Each person will have to observe himself to determine the times of optimum effectiveness.

If prime time comes in the morning, this would appear to be the period for things that require the most concentration: study and sermon writing. At eleven o'clock a change of pace to correspondence and routine tasks may be wise. After lunch and relaxation, with energy renewed, the pastor can attack thorny administrative problems and difficult correspondence. These may be followed by several counseling interviews. Then comes the visiting period, which, of course, may begin earlier when there are no interviews. The period after dinner is a lazy time, and when children are small makes a delightful interlude for telling stories and engaging in bedtime ceremonies. Then come fruitful hours for meetings, visiting, or reading.

It is obvious that this basic schedule, following the fluctuation of energy and alertness, also takes other factors into consideration. In some situations these will differ and the pastor must take the variations into account. They are: the place available for study and conditions affecting it, the particular demands on the minister's time and the priorities he assigns in view of his purposes, the hours when persons are able to come for interviews or receive him in their homes, the schedule of meetings he feels required to attend, and the overall balance of his week.

In his administrative activity the pastor must consider another factor; namely, the significant problem area which should have prime time. The "maldistribution principle," valid in every field of endeavor, affirms that "while most measured results are the cumulative effects of many causes, a small minority of causes contribute to a major share of the total effect. The large majority of causes are responsible for a very small share of the total effect." Some acts are, therefore, strategic; others are relatively unimportant.

The pastor must determine in the light of his purposes which are the significant problem areas where effort will produce maximum results. In most churches the development of leadership is a crucial problem, but it receives attention from ministers only in crisis situations or before annual meetings. Once a pastor decides to devote time to this issue he must determine how to use it. Shall he work over the roll, looking for persons of special gifts and estimating possibilities of growth? Shall he meet frequently with the personnel chairman or committee or get them started on a year-round program? Shall he devise a multitude of modest assignments as training experiences for promising people? Shall he plan board meetings carefully so that learning accompanies discussions of policy? Shall he set up a formal training program? Shall he develop one small Bible study group which may become a vital influence and beget leaders? All these things are good, but one of them is worth more time than the others and some can be omitted without loss. The allocation of the best time is important and so is the use of each available moment. This is only possible if there is thoughtful planning.

3. A Time Budget

The pastor can make a time budget. The first step is prayer. It is important to talk with God about your desire to serve him and to ask for the grace of calm, unhurried intelligence as you seek to relate purpose and action. The second step is to discover how you have been using time. A simple procedure is to work out a weekly time chart and have it duplicated. An $8\frac{1}{2}''$ x $11''$ sheet is ruled with one vertical column for each day of the week. Horizontal lines divide the days into one-hour periods from seven A.M. to eleven P.M. Choose symbols for activities: *D* for devotions, *S* for study and sermon preparation, *R* for reading, *V* for visiting and counseling, *A* for administration, *M* for meetings, and X for free time. For a week or two put a blank chart in the top desk drawer and fill it in as each day goes by.

The third step is to develop a tentative time budget on the chart, using the symbols. It is important that your convictions about the pastor's task be mirrored in this budget. Each morning for a time, after your devotions, you will wish to see how your performance compares with your budget. You will learn to make the budget flexible by exchanging periods where imperatives require this, and to make the budget effective by remembering to exchange periods where some category was shortchanged in an emergency. You will also learn that the tentative budget must be changed in the face of reality. However, since you budget ahead, your purposes may remain in control of your time. The whole process of budget-making will encourage thought about your task and will enable you to establish priorities and identify special problem areas.

4. Saving Time and Energy

Any pastor who examines his use of time thoughtfully may be able to effect savings and increase his effectiveness.

a. He may be trying to do too many things. Perhaps he should ask more frequently, Who else could do this? It is flattering to be asked to speak on many occasions, but often it is not important. The impression that only a clergyman is equipped to give the invocation at a big community dinner or a convention is theologically unsound and needs to be changed. There are aspects of counseling that can be much better handled by Family Service or the family doctor or the welfare department or a good psychiatrist. Most congregations have an older man far better equipped than the minister to help young people with vocational problems. Dedicated women can be trained to make effective pastoral calls on shut-ins and even to give support and encouragement to troubled individuals or families.

Delegation of responsibilities and sharing of opportunities for service may free the minister for other tasks and encourage the growth of other church members. The delegated performance may be better, or if it is not done quite so well, it may be better timed than it could have been if fitted into the minister's schedule. The pastor should carry his share of responsibility in the church at large and in the community, but often he tries to represent the whole church. His task is essentially administrative in this respect, and the value of an administrator increases, not as he does things, but as he gets other people to do things. If he is trying to carry the entire burden himself, he is probably getting in the way as God calls each of his children to meaningful service.

Sometimes this mistake arises from pride. It perverts a sincere Christian concern into easy acceptance of the idea that no one else can be found to perform a task. Sometimes a pastor attempts too much because he hesitates to ask others to perform tasks he considers menial. A less sensitive man often gets into the same position because people he would like to recruit sense, or even are told, that he feels he has more important things to do! What a difference there is between these attitudes and the Biblical recognition that God-given tasks cannot be ranked by importance.

There are occasions, of course, when really unnecessary tasks may occupy a pastor's time because he has not taken the trouble to pray and think about what he is doing in the light of God's purposes for him. A church bulletin, for example, may be a very useful thing, but if there is no one but the minister to prepare and duplicate it, the service may be more enhanced through a few orders pasted in the hymnal, and a sermon on which two or three more hours were spent. Listening to a neurotic for an hour or two each week may seem a fine pastoral service, which could nonetheless be largely dispensed with if the poor soul were enrolled in the right group and given some tasks in which she could forget herself.

b. Emergencies may be taking too much of the pastor's time. He may be running around putting out fires that could have been prevented. Reluctance to face personnel problems may produce an endless chain of critical incidents. The minister cannot always control the situation, but most men have more to do with the quality of leadership around them than they like to admit even to themselves. More careful and adequate supervision may take time but will be less wasteful in the long run than hoping for improvements to happen automatically. The removal of an employee or the replacement of a volunteer may be difficult and unpleasant, but it may save wasted hours in every week and greatly increase the effectiveness of a church.

Fires often spring up in unused buildings – or unused lives. Emergencies are constantly breaking out in a church where nothing much is happening. People come into the life of the congregation thrilled with what Christ has done for them and anxious to express their appreciation and love. If they are not helped to find God's task for them, the devil will find something for idle hands – or tongues – to do, and the pastor will spend frustrating hours clearing up what should never have occurred.

Often one fire is unavoidable, but it need not break out again. The sensitive pastor will often find at the root of an unhappy incident in congregational life the problem of an individual or family. It is a welcome obligation to help the person or family become open to God's remedy, and this will take less time than putting out a succession of fires.

c. " The answer man " would be a just name for some unfortunate pastors. Every question that arises must be referred to them. Time is wasted on the same decision made over and over because they have not taken the trouble to settle a number of questions once and for all. The good administrator seeks to have policies and procedures clearly stated so that any member of the organization can deal with routine questions. This greatly reduces the number of appeals to the administrator or the board. Those which do come should be significant. If exceptions to rules emerge too often, the policies need reexamination. Clear-cut job descriptions for volunteers and employees, well-defined rules for the use of buildings and equipment, simple statements about Sacraments, weddings, funerals, and general pastoral services – all these will save time in the long run.

At an even deeper level, it is important for the pastor to avoid the stance of the answer man. As his people face crisis and difficulty, they can develop dependence upon him rather than upon God. This consumes his time, but much worse, it destroys the relationship that he exists to encourage. A constant goal of the pastor must be a people independent of him in crisis because under his day-by-day leadership they have entered into communion with God. He may not be the best, but the worst, pastor, who builds a reputation that " you can always count on him in the time of trouble."

d. Indecision is a robber of time. Pastors are tempted to put off decisions and this can become a wasteful habit. The same question has to be examined repeatedly. Ingenuity is spent on inventing excuses. Matters are referred to boards and committees, though they are already covered by approved policies. The planning process is indefinitely extended. The minister tells himself he must have more facts when he knows the decision will eventually have to be based on the limited knowledge already available.

Sometimes indecision arises from weariness. The minister has lost his resilience from too many continuous hours on the job. Mind and body need a rest. A play or detective story or a good night's rest, or even a day or two off, will bring a more decisive turn of mind. If these have no effect, a doctor may help. Happily, indecision is usually little more than a bad habit. It can be broken by a self-discipline that rules that pressing questions are to be settled at a chosen hour on the day they come up, or to be docketed for a certain day and hour within a week. If additional information is needed, the process of getting the facts is set in motion at once.

e. Too much tension may be costly in time and efficiency. Most people need to feel a bit keyed up to do their best work. The effective speakers are not the most relaxed ones, nor are many creative persons found among those "who haven't a nerve in their bodies." When this proper stress is accentuated painfully by largely unconscious pressures, the quality of work suffers. Under these circumstances, many pastors maintain the quality of their work at serious cost to themselves in energy, time, or eventual bodily harm. Those who have studied executive performance report that worry or unhealthy stress can rob a man of imagination, foresight, and judgment.

An unfortunate pressure on many pastors is the unconscious but real need to prove that they work hard. They laugh at gibes about their "one-day week," but their tendency to overwork and to talk about it suggests that they do not really find this remark very funny. A second unhealthy pressure arises from inferiority feelings that have no relation to actuality. The man consistently undervalues all he is doing and must be forever proving that he is worth his salary. He is uneasy about fellow workers, since their successes threaten him and their failures reflect on his judgment in having chosen them. A third vicious pressure is that of perfectionism, which, in the face of lifelong experience, blindly demands ideal performance of self and others. This would be comic in a pastor if it were not tragic, since he is coach of a team that exists to proclaim God's grace to imperfect men. But, many pastors suffer from perfectionism.

Every one of us will do well once in a while to talk this over with God in the devotional hour; with his help examining stresses with an eye for disease, a mind open for correction, and a heart ready to receive grace. Occasionally, the pastor may need to talk with a trusted friend, become part of a small group in which a person may relax defenses and see himself as he is, or consult a physician.

Chapter III

Planning

Planning is the first step in administration. It is not possible for a group of people to do anything together until someone visualizes what is to be done, and then breaks the task down into manageable segments.

Jesus did this in the days of his flesh. He encountered temptations in the wilderness as he prayerfully made long-range plans for his own life. From beginning to end it is clear that he clarified his purposes, examined alternative courses of action, made clear-cut decisions, and broke his plan down into sequential steps. There is a logical consistency in his actions that could not have arisen by chance. The announcement of his mission, the choice of the Twelve, the ambiguity of his claims until his character was known, the training missions of the Twelve and the Seventy, the alternation of attack and retreat, the careful preparation for the events of the Passion Week, all these things and countless others indicate careful planning. It is obvious from his behavior that his warning against taking thought for the morrow has to do with nervous concern about things that cannot be anticipated, not with sensible planning in the spirit of prayer and of humble dependence upon the Father.

1. Elements in Planning

Effective planning is an orderly process involving six steps: clarification of purposes, analysis of the situation, development of possible lines of action, decision, outlining a detailed program, and preparation of a pattern of action. This is a chain that connects purposes with results. Each link is important.

a. *Clarification of Purposes.* The proliferation of meaningless activity in many churches cries out for greater attention to purposes. We have agreed that the church is a fellowship of love that exists for worship, mutual nurture, and witness. These purposes must shape its life. It is important that they never be forgotten by a group that is making plans for a congregation.

Each local church, like each Christian, is in a particular place and time, endowed with some gifts and without others, faced with particular opportunities and problems. Its fulfillment of the general purposes of the church will be conditioned by these things. A careful statement of the purposes of the group meeting on one corner may therefore differ somewhat from that of groups in other circumstances. Perhaps the worship of this group should be enriched with all the treasures of the ages and embellished with the finest contributions of contemporary art and music, while another group should worship in a storefront and keep everything stark and simple. Possibly one church must set forth the eternal message in the kinds of preaching and teaching that will appeal to students and professional people, while a second congregation must direct its evangel to folks hardly literate, and a third must devise presentations that will reach an incredibly diverse group. Witness in a particular place may require a weekly radio program or a migrant ministry, an elaborate visitation program or informal gatherings in homes, a breakfast prayer group or a militant committee on housing. All these things may be appropriate in one church and wildly absurd in another.

One church should grow each year, while another should be an entrance gate that feeds members into other churches, and a third church serves best in living under a strict discipline that attracts only a few intrepid souls. A congregation of one sort should be expressing its witness in huge financial contributions to the world mission of the church, while a group in a different neighborhood should devote the bulk of its income to desperate needs immediately at hand. Whatever its circumstance, the local church is under obligation to refine and state its purposes when it makes its plans.

b. *Analysis of the Situation.* The second element in planning is an analysis of the situation based on all the information available.

The planners will wish to ask how well the present program

relates to the purposes of the church. No organization or activity should be spared a searching examination in this connection. The church cannot afford to waste energy on things that have no relation to Christian fellowship in worship or mutual nurture or witness. There may be a study of the participation of members in the present program, its effect on those who take part, and the reasons others do not. Trends in congregational life related to such things as age groups and birthrate may be charted to anticipate future opportunities and problems.

Facts about the community may be assembled. The planners will be interested in rates and directions of change and their implications. They will study the problems and potentials of the immediate neighborhood as well as the larger community. Special attention will be given to unreached people. A religious survey of the area may be attempted, preferably in concert with the other churches. Some desirable information will not be available. Possible relocations of population and arteries of traffic may await unpredictable political action. Income estimates will be subject to fluctuations in the economy. Useful studies or surveys may be too expensive in time or money. Whatever the circumstances, planners should be aware of what they do not know, and evaluate its importance. They will then have an index of the degree of probability on which projections are based.

In analyzing the situation with facts in hand, planners will have to ask: (1) whether the specific purposes they have developed should be changed in any way in view of the facts, (2) what conditions are favorable to the purposes of the church, (3) what problems are posed by the situation or by likely changes, (4) what special opportunities and needs confront the church.

c. *Development of Possible Lines of Action.* The third element in planning, depending on the purposes and situation, will involve research on what others have done or are doing. Beyond this, creative imagination must develop a maximum number of possibilities and bring them together with the ideas of others into courses of action which could be suggested. The planners should work over each line of action, noting its advantages and difficulties, its cost in time and energy, and its feasibility in view of resources at hand or obtainable. They may then arrange alternatives in order of desirability, which is determined by balancing advantages and disadvantages of each, and putting the one with the most favorable balance at the top.

d. *Decision.* This is the crucial fourth step. The quality of the choice will be largely dependent on clarity of purposes and situation and the soundness of the alternative lines of action proposed. No strong decision is likely if it is not possible to weigh the relative merits of several live options. However, a decision upon a line of action is of the essence of planning, and there comes a time when delay for further refinement of possibilities can be disastrous. A good planner recognizes this moment by balancing the consequences of delay with the advantages to be gained from new information or ideas. He knows that man can never have certainty. When he has done his best he must act in faith.

e. *Outlining a Program in Detail.* When a course of action is chosen, it must be broken down into step-by-step objectives, with an outline of definite projects, meetings, and activities. Anything human beings are to do must be divided into segments for action. The outline of a total church program will be treated in Part Two.

f. *Preparing a Pattern of Action.* Once the program is outlined, a pattern of action must be developed. This involves: (1) a clear-cut organization in which responsibilities and relationships are plainly spelled out (Chapter IV), (2) the recruiting and training of personnel (Chapters V and VI), and (3) ways of working with groups (Chapter VII).

2. Group Planning

Plans for a church may be made by an individual or worked out in a group. It is obvious that a group will not be as effective as an individual in gathering detailed information and carrying on research, or in framing a working paper. However, there are distinct advantages in having a group do as much of the planning as possible.

a. *Reasons for Group Planning.* The convening of the Jerusalem Council reported in the book of The Acts says plainly that the apostles, on the basis of Jesus' teaching, expected the

Holy Spirit to guide the church through the voice of a representative group. They remembered his words, " Where two or three are gathered together in my name, there am I in the midst." They recalled that it was to the group of disciples he had said, " Receive ye the Holy Ghost," and that when the Spirit came with Pentecostal power it was to an assembled group.

Christians of every age, being aware that God speaks to others at least as clearly as he speaks to them, have recognized a divine authority in group decisions on such subjects as the canon of Scripture, the definition of central Christian truth, and ways of administering the church in a particular time. It is not that fallible human beings become infallible in a group, nor that an individual may not occasionally be nearer to God's will than a company of people. It is that God has given us reason, except in the face of weighty evidence, to subject ourselves to the assembled brethren.

That God knew what he was about in arranging things this way is clear from general human experience. In the corrupted currents of this world it does not take long to discover that individual choices are invariably tainted by self-interest and limited perspective. This is true of Christians as of other people, for perfection is beyond us all on earth. Decisions reached by democratic procedures involve a balancing of interests that is usually fairer to all. The consensus also brings together varied perspectives in a view likely to be richer and deeper. Further, the motivation to work is increased by participation in planning. Industrial practices have been affected by this discovery, and the church would be foolish to ignore it even if it had not more important reasons for group planning.

b. *Procedures in Group Planning.* A planning consultant or chairman may be elected or appointed by the official board (or congregation). If he is a chairman, there will be a planning committee. If he is a consultant, the board, itself, will act at times as a planning committee. The consultant or the planning committee will be available to the pastor for discussion of planning or may take the initiative and ask the pastor's cooperation.

When a group is to take part in planning, it will be helpful to follow these steps, all applicable to long-range or annual or special planning. The early steps will be simplified in annual planning, after the first year, or following development of a long-range plan.

(1) The consultant or chairman or if need be at first, the pastor, brings to the group a paper on purposes. When this has been discussed, the person who brought it to them may be in a position to put the fruits of the meeting into a clear statement of purposes for approval at the next meeting.

(2) The individual may then be asked to bring the group a written analysis of the church's situation, with supporting facts. The writer may elicit the cooperation of many persons and groups in obtaining information. He may use a *Self Study Guide* prepared for churches by a denominational service agency.

(3) When this report analyzing the situation is presented to the group, discussion may bring out new facts or unnoticed implications of the material at hand or the need for further information. Additional research and reports to subsequent meetings may be necessary.

(4) When agreement has been reached as to the facts of the situation and their meaning, the individual may be asked to develop possible courses of action. In meeting this assignment, he may enlist the help of other members and outside experts.

(5) His report on possible lines of action may be discussed by the group. Other alternatives may emerge and require reference for notation as to their difficulties and advantages.

(6) When the group is satisfied that all possibilities have been considered, they must choose the best course of action.

(7) Someone may then be commissioned to outline a program and a pattern of action.

(8) When these have been discussed, revised, referred, and approved in final form, the planning is completed.

c. *Participants in Group Planning.* Usually, planning will be the responsibility of *the official board* of a congregation. This may differ according to church law in various communions. Some boards will prefer to have a small committee prepare the papers for each step before bringing them to the whole group. Some will feel it wise to convene all the officers of the congregation and its varied groups for *a planning con-*

ference. In this case steps " 1 " through " 5 " are usually taken in advance by the board. The planning conference is then asked to consider the alternatives in the light of the church's purposes and situation, and recommend a course of action, leaving to the board the task of working out the detailed program and pattern.

Sometimes, especially when extensive changes or large expenditures of energy or money may be involved, the planning conference meets three times. First, it discusses a report on purposes and situation. Second, it considers and acts on recommendations for possible lines of action. Third, it examines and acts on suggestions for program and pattern. In some instances it may be wise to involve the entire congregation in the discussion at one, or all three, of these points.

3. Long-Range Planning

Long-range planning develops a framework within which other planning is done; it keeps action related to purposes and situation; it anticipates needs and leads to an orderly congregational life. Usually, the elements in the plan are set forth in a paper that is in the hands of all board members and organization officers. This paper covers the next ten years in broad outline, with detail on the nearer years. It is revised annually.

4. Planning the Church Year

Planning for a year beginning in September should be completed in June. The planning committee first asks someone to prepare a brief *outline of the year* showing special Sundays and seasons. When they are satisfied with this, they begin to prepare two detailed charts. One covers an 8½″ x 11″ sheet with an oblong of 28 squares, 7 squares wide and 4 squares high, showing a typical month. It is obvious at a glance that each of the 28 squares represents a particular day of the month, such as first Monday or third Friday. The services and meetings regularly scheduled on a certain day of each month are noted in the proper square with the hours at which they occur. The result is a clear outline of regular weekly and monthly activities. The committee prepares a second chart which, in simple outline form, divided into months and following a date sequence, presents activities that do not occur monthly, as well as special projects. When they make these charts for the first time the committee members rely on the church bulletins or newsletters of previous years, plus their own projections. Then they send the two charts, marked "preliminary," to the officers of all organizations for corrections and suggestions. In subsequent years they send out copies of the current charts, asking confirmation of the schedule or proposed changes for the coming year by a certain date. At that time they confer with groups to eliminate conflicting plans, then prepare revised editions of the two charts to be submitted for official board approval. In some churches the official board calls a planning conference, including officers of all organizations, and asks for their approval of the completed charts. This helps to build morale, elicits creative ideas before the program is hardened, and eliminates complaints when sudden inspirations during the year cannot be fitted into the schedule. The committee sends mimeographed copies of the approved charts to all officers and groups.

A proposed financial budget will be in process during June and completed by September 15 if there is to be a canvass in November. Budget-making is a part of the planning process. It has an obvious effect on the church program. The individuals charged with shaping the budget for board (and congregational) approval should participate in the rest of the planning process. Where more than one board has some responsibility for aspects of the budget, representatives of each, and of the canvass committee, should sit in on budget preparation.

5. Planning a Building Campaign

A church board anticipating a building campaign may follow the planning process up to the third element, "Development of Possible Lines of Action." At this point, without retaining anyone, they may wish to seek advice from an architect, and, if the project will cost more than the annual budget, of a professional fund raiser. Once a decision to build has been made, they will need to retain these professionals for help as they work out the details of program and organization and the building plans. If the plan to build emerges as an aspect of long-range planning, the tasks of all will be easier, and success more likely.

6. Choosing a Site for a Church

The choice of location will be based on the needs of an area and the mission of the church. Needs may be determined by a house-to-house survey. This should be preceded by census tract studies, which will indicate the character of the population, the birthrate, and the long-term direction of changes. Also helpful are estimates of population trends by utility companies, which base heavy investments on their opinions. Plans of builders for developments including many houses must be judged in the light of their past performances and in the light of separately obtained information about availability of water and sewage facilities and applicability of zoning laws. The character and number of churches already in or near the area must be weighed, with attention to the denominational preferences of those canvassed. Comity committees of councils of churches, where they exist, may offer guidance, and their allocations of areas should be respected.

The mission of the church to be established must be clear. What constituency does it intend to serve? What programs will be essential? In view of these, will a site available within the price range have adequate space? For an inner-city church this may be a twenty-foot front in a block; for a suburban church, five acres. What about accessibility? Will its potential members pass it often enough to know where it is? Will they be able to walk to it, or reach it by public transportation, or park nearby if they come by car?

7. Deciding Whether to Move a Church

a. *A Downtown Church.* A downtown church may find itself completely surrounded by business and industry. Abandonment of the old site requires serious consideration of the community needs and the mission of the church. It must determine by survey how many persons live within walking distance. Other inquiries will be addressed to the availability of public transportation, present and projected freeways to bring traffic downtown, possible parking facilities, and new trends to apartment living downtown. There may be a ministry to people nearby who have not been noticed. It may be possible to develop a fellowship that includes all kinds of people from every part of the city and its suburbs. In many urban areas a downtown church provides the most inclusive fellowship and the only lifelong relationships for people who start in a small apartment and change neighborhoods as they move up the social and economic ladder. Such a church frequently has talented people who may together develop a program well worth a little extra travel. It will train many members who will go to other churches in time and give leadership. It will minister during the week to those who work near it. It will seek a pastor of outstanding gifts whose preaching and leadership will make an impact on the city.

The only sound reasons for abandoning a downtown site are total inaccessibility, resources too limited to attempt an effective program, or other churches better prepared to perform an adequate ministry. No city should be left without at least one strong downtown church, even if this means the use of denominational resources.

b. *Neighborhood Churches.* A neighborhood church may be inclined to move if it is in a deteriorating area like the inner city, the blighted ring just beyond the center. Relocation is justified if a study shows there are too many churches and a united strategy designates some to stay and others to go. Frequently a deteriorating neighborhood has more people than before, but they are different. The differences may be those of race or national origin, education or custom, income or experience of responsibility, age or state of health. Sometimes the people of an area simply grow old together, while the more prosperous ones move away. The church is left with a shrinking income to deal creatively with the problems of the aged. In the more disorganized communities houses are cut up, many people live on public assistance, crime threatens, and families move frequently. A public school may have a complete change of pupils in the course of each year, and a third of the children may come to classes hungry, largely because of parental ineptitude and lack of foresight.

A church may have a creative ministry in this chaos, but it may need members who live in other districts or substantial help from other churches in the form of regular workers and money. Increasingly, Christians moving from these neighborhoods are feeling an obligation to continue part of the fellowship ministering there. At the same time, suburban churches are working out plans for members to be " loaned " for creative ministries as temporary " members " of neighborhood congregations. These developments are healthy evidences of real Christian fellowship and concern, but care must be taken that local members have opportunity for as much leadership as they can provide, and except in the most disorganized communities, self-support should be a goal. If any possibility of continuing ministry exists, the neighborhood church cannot conscientiously leave hungry sheep. Fortunately, the decision to stay is made easier because many of the ablest seminary graduates want to work in these demanding situations.

c. *Suburban and Town Churches.* Occasionally these churches consider moving. Conditions may affect their accessibility, or a price may be offered for their property which will enable them to have much better facilities nearby. There may be need for additional space now limited by zoning laws or property size. A study may indicate that there are too many churches, and an agreed strategy may call for one to move. These are largely questions of prudence. Sound answers should follow study and evaluation.

d. *Rural Churches.* Churches in rural areas often face a shrinking population. Personal and financial support or an effective program seems to call for consolidation of churches into larger units, or the use of " larger parish plans." Modern transportation makes this practical. The few young people who remain in some areas particularly need a wider fellowship. However, traditional loyalties are strong, community pride has some legitimacy, social and economic differences are real, and the close-knit little congregation has values. The comparative importance of these things must be weighed in the light of the purposes of the church. Frequently, consolidation at population centers is the best way for the Christian people of a rural area to realize their common life in Christ. It may be possible to conserve the best in rural experience by using programs such as the house church or other ideas yet unborn, or by carrying on some functions in scattered meetinghouses and some at a central location. It may also be possible to increase the percentage of the population included in the churches through programs that seem to have more relevance.

CHAPTER IV

Organization

Organizing is the process of defining and grouping the activities of an enterprise, establishing the responsibilities and relationships of the persons involved, in order to accomplish the ends of the group.

1. THE CHARACTER AND RESULTS OF GOOD ORGANIZATION

The goal of organization is a structure adapted to its ends, efficient and easily understood by all participants. The organizer takes seriously Paul's statement, " Now ye are the body of Christ, and members [or organs] in particular " (I Cor. 12:27). He goes about his task aware that the body is at its best when all the organs are able to perform their divinely intended functions. He knows that the proper arrangement of organs – or organization – is God's doing, but that in this, as in other things, he uses human agency under the guidance of his Spirit. The sound structure that emerges opens the way for each member of the church to exercise fruitfully the particular gifts he has received from God. Only then does the universal priesthood of all believers take substance. Good organization opens the way for healthy relations between the members, and for a proper subordination of all the members and their groups to the Head of the body, Jesus Christ.

a. *Order* emerges in place of confusion. Individuals see their places in the life of the church. Groups understand why they exist. Activities have meaning. Ends are clearly distinguished from means. People are guarded against idolatry – that devotion to human forms and structures in which loyalty is given to scaffolding. It is not because of too much organization, but as a result of inadequate organization, that structures are developed for structures' sake, or the preservation of some class or association, exactly as it has always been, is considered a great service to God.

b. *Efficiency* is a product of good organization which is the enemy of waste. Coordination avoids duplication of effort. Without it, several groups may try to accomplish the same things, or work at cross-purposes. Strategic thinking leads to concentration of strength where it counts. Capable people do important things and are spared fruitless efforts. Outmoded structures are allowed to wither. New structures are erected only when none exists to perform a function. Avoided are detailed group constitutions, overelaborate records, officers and meetings unrelated to the purpose of the church. Attention is focused on real needs and opportunities for service.

c. *Participation* of members in the common life of the fellowship, and in its mission, is a product of good organization. There is a place for each in some aspect of the church's work. Tasks within the walls and those in the community are considered in making assignments. The whole lives of individuals are considered in recruiting so that " church work " does not sound the knell of devotional and family life, and is not narrowly conceived. Arrangements are made for some to serve the church beyond the local scene through denominational and ecumenical channels, and for all to carry a form of witness in the community, through vocational or avocational tasks.

When little attention is given to organization a congregation tends to become an audience. At the center of one city such an audience gathered week by week to hear a preacher with a " silver tongue." When he departed after twenty years to preach in another city, he left behind a reputation for eloquence, and some loyal friends, but little else. His successor found nothing much but a church building. He was a good preacher and worked hard at his sermons, but he also gave attention to the corporate life of the congregation and spent time in organizing. Although the city lost population during the twenty-five years of his service and the church supplied leadership for a number of new churches in the suburbs, the church became a vital fellowship under his ministry. Outward signs of growth were unmistakable: a tripled attendance at worship, a doubled membership, twice as many boys and girls in the church school during a period of declining birthrate, and great increases in giving to the mission enterprise. Those who knew these people at close range could tell of other things: family worship in more than half the homes; every parent participating in Christian education; burgeoning youth groups with obvious effects on the lives of members; a new social consciousness that led members of the church into leadership in unnumbered community activities; the development of patterns of church life now in use across the country. When he died this minister left his successor a strong family of God centered in Christ and ready for new adventures in his service. The key to his effectiveness was pastoral organizing which resulted in wide participation.

Group structures that encourage wide participation also militate against the development of dictatorial practices on the part of one or two. Monopolies of influence and nepotism are made difficult, as are the formation of cliques, and temptations to sub-Christian exclusiveness or manipulation of persons.

The growth of individuals is another wonderful result of arrangements for every member to take a part in the life of the church. In one city a single church has trained a large proportion of the ablest civic leadership. Its members are at work in politics, education, business, finance, social improvement, charity, and world concern. Scores of these people would have done little had they not first been involved in active service through the organized life of the church. In another situation an almost inarticulate bus driver was drawn into the active life of the fellowship and developed extraordinary ability to win men and women to Christ. His ministry reached others like himself – and the head of a vast industry who became a close friend. This came about because of good organization.

d. *Contingency* is a characteristic of sound structure in the church. Everyone involved needs to be aware of this. The organization takes form as the people of God try to order their common life under the leading of the divine Word of love and power in Christ, in the midst of the contemporary situation. The circumstances never remain the same. God, who is not bound by old patterns, may require quite different orders of life in various times and places. Karl Barth is quite right in warning us to sit loose to all forms of organization so that " all encroachment on the Lordship of the One who is alone Lord is either avoided, or so suppressed and eliminated in practice, that there is place for his rule."

In practical terms this means a constant reexamination — as in annual planning conferences — of current organization. Christians who do this must be daily open to the Word that God may speak to them through Scripture to guide their life together in the changing world. It means that some of them will devote time to study of Scripture and the contemporary scene, asking questions about order in the church and hoping to share with the brethren what they believe God has to say. It means that no form of organization is to be regarded as sacred or permanent, and no structure as important as a person who may live forever.

2. Factors in Good Organization

a. *Clear arrangement* is essential. If organization is to be effective, it must be coherent and everyone involved must understand it. A constitution or set of bylaws may be necessary. Where these are not provided by denominational law, suggested forms are available from headquarters. Where bylaws must be written for the first time, it will be easier to do so after working out an organization chart.

(1) *An organization chart* or outline has advantages in any event: (*a*) The preparation itself requires development of clear assignments. (*b*) Inconsistencies or omissions are quickly apparent and may be corrected. (*c*) When changes are suggested, it is easier to see how they fit into the structure and what their effect will be. (*d*) Everyone can grasp the plan.

(2) *Job descriptions* are increasingly used in churches. These consist of brief, but exact expositions of each task: membership on a board or committee, an office or chairmanship, an employed status. Values are obvious: (*a*) The preparation of job descriptions requires clear thinking about each assignment. (*b*) A person may consider acceptance of a position intelligently. (*c*) One does not waste a long period discovering what he is supposed to do. (*d*) One may be aware of the extent and limits of his own job description and those of others working with him.

b. *The span of leadership* requires attention. A leader in organizational activity can work directly only with a limited number of persons. In business and the army, this span has been found to be effective with four to eight persons at upper levels, and up to twenty-five persons where simple manual operations are performed. Depth studies of groups in action have made it apparent that the relationships that develop are very complicated. There is interaction not only between individuals but between pairs and pairs, pairs and individuals, threes and threes, threes and pairs, threes and individuals, and so on. The total number of possible relationships when a leader works with one other person is one; with two persons, six; with four persons, forty-four; with ten persons, 5,210. Fortunately not all of these potentials develop, but enough do evolve to make the leader's task less than simple. The difficulty increases with the number of persons working directly together and the number of responsibilities in which they share. This means that in a good organization a leader works directly with a limited number of other leaders or workers. If he is expected to deal immediately with too many persons his area falls into disorder from lack of direction or he becomes a " bottleneck," slowing everything down. This may be observed in more than one church.

The obvious solution is to limit the number of major leaders with whom a pastor or church officer or committee chairman works. This will affect the number of boards and committees, their structure and size. The leveling that occurs when this is done in a larger church may have serious disadvantages. Some people may feel that their jobs are unimportant because they do not work directly with the " chief." Effective communication is never easy through second and third persons. The structure itself may be cumbersome and demand too much time for maintenance. Experience and practice in churches suggest that for any more or less permanent structure, there should not be more than two levels in addition to the leader. Thus a pastor or board chairman may work primarily with committee chairmen, who in turn work directly with the board members all assigned to committees. He presides at executive committee meetings as well as at board meetings, but need not ordinarily attend committee meetings.

More levels are practicable for campaign organizations designed for one major assignment in evangelism or fund-raising. Multilevel structures are sometimes set up for continuing service as in the case of neighborhood plans for pastoral oversight, with area leaders, division leaders, section leaders, and block leaders. Usually, they fall soon of their own weight or require a full-time secretary.

c. *Authority and responsibility* must be understood. Responsibility is the obligation to see that something happens or does not happen. It may be shared, but cannot be delegated. The man who publicly blames his secretary or an associate for a failure in his area shows that he does not understand the nature of responsibility. Sharing it does not reduce it in the least.

Authority is the right to use necessary means to get things done. It may be delegated and its limits may be defined. Once given, it may be revoked, but while it stands, attempts to share it lead to confusion and frustration. A pastor or board chairman creates havoc when he takes action on a matter previously referred to a music committee or a board of Christian education. A leader who assigns a project to someone else and then takes a hand in it without the other's invitation, or changes the conditions without consultation, does not understand the nature of authority, or violates it.

The parts of God's ultimate responsibility and authority required for performance of the tasks he assigns are understood by most Protestants to be shared with, and delegated to, the fellowship of Christians. This group in turn passes them on to chosen officers or boards. The official board, variously named and constituted, becomes the center of responsibility and fount of authority, except for a few matters reserved for the congregation as a whole, such as the call of a minister or the approval of a budget.

In many denominations, a constitution spells out the responsibility and authority of the congregation, board or boards, and members. It reserves some powers for the whole fellowship represented in church courts, or officials beyond the local scene. The official board of the church on the corner may choose to carry this still farther by sharing responsibility for particular tasks with specific boards or committees or individuals, and granting them the necessary authority to perform these functions. Bylaws, organization charts, and job descriptions represent policy decisions in these matters.

d. *Size* is an important consideration in organizing. The ideal size for a church is not easily determined. The question must be answered in terms of purposes and resources.

(1) *Smallness* has the advantage of face-to-face relationships in which each member knows the others and may share in their lives. It also makes possible a very simple organization. It has the disadvantage of providing extremely limited resources for effective programs of worship, nurture, and witness. It tends to be minister-centered because there may be no one else equipped to do many things. It is wasteful of ministerial time and if a general pattern of very small churches developed, it would be necessary to increase the number of pastors many times. It produces an institution that compares unfavorably with those institutions involved in education, business, and politics, suggesting that the latter are more important.

(2) *Bigness* is a bad word in our time, but it has some real advantages. The large church can develop excellent programs of worship, nurture, and witness. It has a wide variety of gifts in its membership and can provide opportunities for every sort of person. It may bring together in Christian fellowship persons of very different backgrounds who need to learn how to live together. It may use the financial resources of many members to engage in a wide ministry on many fronts at home and abroad. It usually makes effective use of ministerial time, employing an average of one pastor for each six hundred members.

The most serious charge against largeness is that it makes real fellowship impossible. This is true and it holds for any church with more than twenty-five members! A few pointed inquiries will show that the vaunted intimacy of churches of one or two hundred is skin deep, except for a small inner circle. It is difficult to live in openness with more than a dozen people, as Jesus knew. The idea that " everyone in our church knows everyone else " is an illusion. The obvious solution to this problem is the development, within the larger group, of many small groups who really do know each other and care about each other. These are more likely to develop in the larger church where there is more leadership. Something of this sort must have occurred in the first Christian church which received three thousand members on the day it was founded in Jerusalem.

In view of these considerations, it would appear that except where population is widely scattered, or rapidly growing, or where a special ministry may be performed, there would seem to be no good reason to plan for congregations of less than three hundred persons. One pastor may serve three to seven hundred members well, and many will choose this as the best size range. They prefer to have one man perform all the ministerial functions. They believe that an official board of six to fourteen, with one member for each fifty in the congregation will be about the right size. They think there will be a fellowship wide enough, and adequate resources.

The church of eight hundred to several thousand which employs more than one minister, and has great personal and physical resources, is attractive to a good number of people. Because of the rapid growth of population, pastoral service in multiple-staff churches is increasing faster than any other form of ministerial activity. Many ministers and members are convinced that the larger institution, given the right organization and leadership, may best perform the mission of the church. The larger boards necessary to assure adequate representation may achieve effectiveness through a sound committee structure. Emphasis on small groups may overcome any drift toward impersonality.

The question of congregational size deserves further study. We will all be indebted to the man who develops meaningful categories for comparisons and engages in a sound research project on the effect of size. In the meanwhile, it is obvious that churches will continue to exist in many sizes, though population increases will press toward larger congregations which must have effective organization if they are to perform their essential functions.

3. Forms of Organization

a. *Central organization* is essential if the purposes of the church are to control its activities, and these are to go forward in harmonious effectiveness.

(1) *The official board* usually has a form established by denominational law or practice. Sometimes there is provision for several boards, one with ecclesiastical authority, one with predominantly secular tasks, others with specific responsibilities such as the welfare task assigned to Presbyterian deacons. Whatever the arrangement, it is essential that authority be vested in one official board, and that this be clear to everyone. This board may delegate certain powers to groups that may be

called boards or commissions or departments or committees. It is helpful if the chairmen or some members of these subsidiary groups are members of the official board. If this is impractical, the pastor will wish to attend each board meeting and act as liaison. His time is conserved if the separate groups, whatever their names, are essentially committees of the one official board, their chairmen appointed from this board and reporting to it each month. It is important that the powers and functions of the subsidiary boards or committees be clearly spelled out, and that authority once delegated, be not usurped. The advantage of calling them boards lies in the implied importance of membership in them, which may attract more gifted members. The disadvantage is the temptation to assume autonomy, which may give rise to unnecessary conflict.

(2) *The structure* of a central organization may be set forth in a diagram. If this is not possible, the organization needs clarification. Each church works out its own detailed organization with variations permitted by denominational patterns. The form of an organization chart will depend upon the designer's purpose. Charts may connect groups with lines to clarify responsibilities and relationships. Sometimes they are made in pie shape or with interlocking circles to stress overlapping concerns or to emphasize the equal importance of functioning groups and staff members related to them.

Organization charts may be changed as different needs emerge or new approaches seem desirable. Changes in the employed staff may offer sound reasons for merging two departments into one or dividing a department or reassigning functions. Staff service is likely to be more effective if the same employee assists with all the responsibilities of a commission or department. This, of course, does not imply that one person may not work with several departments, nor that he may not require help from other staff members in a particular department.

(3) *An executive committee* of the official board is needed when the board is large. It may consist of the officers and commission chairmen. It should prepare board dockets, be responsible for planning and for emergency decisions, and may act as a staff committee to deal with employees.

(4) *Commissions* may meet monthly and cover the general program area assigned. They may have standing committees

for some of the specific areas and appoint special committees for others, as necessary. " Span of Leadership " experience suggests that there should not be more than eight commissions. The eight recommended in this book may be reduced to five by combinations of the membership and evangelism commissions, the Christian education and church and society commissions, and the property and finance commissions. A further reduction to four commissions may be effected by eliminating the stewardship commission and dividing its responsibilities between Christian education and property and finance.

The worship commission may be responsible for services, Sacraments, music, and ushering. If there is an ushers' association, its chairman serves on the commission and reports to it regularly. Usually, there is a music committee which meets regularly. A few churches have a separate music commission or department.

The membership commission may be responsible for pastoral care, spiritual life, and the history of the church. A board of deacons or service board may carry responsibility for pastoral visitation and for meeting welfare needs. Its president serves on the commission. Sometimes this board takes the place of the membership commission. Under these circumstances, " history," and sometimes " spiritual life," may be assigned to the Christian education commission.

The evangelism commission may be responsible for visitations and other evangelistic activities, the assimilation of new members, public relations, and the church's world mission. An invitation committee may do much of the evangelistic visiting, with its chairman serving on the commission. Sometimes there is one commission covering the responsibilities listed under membership and evangelism. It may take one of these names or be known as the commission on parish life.

The Christian education commission is often known, instead, as the board of Christian education. It may have responsibility for educational work with children, young people, and adults, special courses and programs, leadership education, resources and techniques, conferences and camps, and religious arts. There may be a youth council composed of representatives from the young people's organizations. An adult council may include representatives of the women's association, the men's club, the couples groups, the spiritual life groups, and various classes of all sorts. A religious arts council may bring together those persons interested in developing programs and festivals of the arts. Chairmen of these councils should serve on the commission and report to it.

The stewardship commission may work in the areas of vocation, personnel, stewardship education, and the Every Member Canvass. *The church and society commission* may be responsible for study and research, social education and action projects. *The property commission* may be charged with building maintenance, housekeeping, insurance and safety.

The finance commission may be responsible for finances and legal business. In many churches a board of trustees takes the place of the last two commissions and has committees on property, finance, legal matters, and insurance and safety. A number of states require that a congregation elect a board of trustees to hold church property. When there is to be a unicameral official board, those persons elected to the board must also be elected as trustees. In states that limit the number of trustees, only some of those elected to a large official board are also elected trustees. When there is a separate board of trustees it is wise for the official board to delegate to this board certain powers and to review their use from time to time. The only authority granted trustees by state law is that of holding title to church property which may only be used or mortgaged or sold at congregational direction.

(5) *The rotary system* should apply to membership in the official board and all commissions and offices. Members should be elected for three years in annual classes of equal size, and should be ineligible for reelection to the same position after two three-year terms, until at least a year has elapsed. A static church board soon ceases to be representative and often lacks dynamism as well. Official board members released from their tenure may bring their experience to the commissions and to other organizations. When they return to the board they will be better prepared to serve them.

b. *Organizations* within the life of the church may elect their own officers, devise their own programs, and even have separate budgets. They can be very important fellowships through which the purposes of the church are fulfilled. They can also develop in ways that involve wasted effort and conflict.

(1) *The church school* may have begun as a separate organization and may continue to function as a separate entity. Usually this is contrary to denominational law and deprives the official board of effective direction of the program of nurture. It may result in conflicting policies and a confused program. The devoted interest of those persons identified with this organization may ordinarily be conserved by their inclusion in the Christian education commission or board at the time it is organized under the authority of the official board.

(2) *Adult Bible classes* may be separate organizations. Some have extensive programs of fellowship and witness in addition to class sessions. A few have even erected buildings on the church plot! They may carry forward very precious relationships that support and encourage members in their Christian living. Church officers will wish to encourage these groups, and at the same time to relate them to the official structure, in the interests of harmony and effectiveness. Steps may be taken in this direction as the classes seek help in recruiting members and securing teachers. Several well-known leaders of the adult classes may be appointed by the official board to the Christian education commission. In establishing new classes, it may be well to provide for minimal organization and no separate budget except for refreshments and incidentals.

(3) *Choirs* may take organizational form for the encouragement of attendance, morale and discipline, care of music and robes, and development of fellowship. The official board, which is responsible for worship, will wish to choose the choir director and hold him accountable for the choice of music. Where usage has established participation of the choir in the selection of a director, or of music, the director is in an impossible position. The situation should be tactfully, but firmly, changed by the official board. The change may be more acceptable if several able members of the choir are appointed members of the music committee to which the official board delegates authority in this field.

(4) *Youth groups* may be separately organized. It is good experience for young people to devise their own plans for carrying forward the purposes of the church, and to participate in all aspects of Christian activity. It is essential that in this process they have sympathetic advisers who will make available to them the long experience of the church, without at-

tempting to make decisions for the group. The adviser's task needs to be clearly defined so that the individual or couple and the group have the same expectations. This job description will vary with different age groups, the element of authority diminishing to the vanishing point at the young adult level.

A second necessity is a relation to the whole congregation through the official structure. This may be achieved through the appointment of one or two of the young people to the Christian education commission. In larger churches there may be a *youth council* composed of officers or representatives from each youth fellowship. This council will have powers delegated through the board of Christian education.

A third matter of importance is primary loyalty to the church of which the group is an arm, lest young people grow up with a fragmentary conception of the church. Like adults, young people may secure help from, and give strength to, denominational, interdenominational, and nondenominational movements, and a number of secular agencies. These relationships may be encouraged as long as the organizations involved do not seek to take the place of the local church, and as long as their purposes are consistent with those of the church.

(5) *Women's organizations* may be independent, federated, or unified in one structure. Independent organizations grew up in many churches to meet definite needs. The ladies aid society assisted the officers in housekeeping, charity, and fund-raising. The women's missionary society prayed for missionaries, provided for their personal needs, and raised surprisingly large sums for their support. The sewing circle made garments and other necessities for missions and for the poor at home. The devotion and sacrifice elicited by these groups did much to strengthen the ministry of each congregation. However, the separate organizations often competed with other groups and even with the church, itself, for allegiance from church members and tended to aggravate one-sided inclinations in particular women. Such organizations sometimes became cherished centers of power in congregational life and fostered pride and aggression. It was difficult to coordinate efforts, and energy was wasted in actions at cross-purposes.

A federated plan was developed to preserve the values of the separate organizations and overcome some of their liabilities. Each group was represented on a women's board. This board met monthly for coordination of activities. The regular association opened the eyes of the leaders to their common interests, and the value of their separate functions. The board frequently took responsibility for promoting membership in all the groups. When new tasks emerged, or requests came from the official board, they were referred to the proper group. Sometimes it was apparent that no group had sufficient personnel or resources to undertake a responsibility. A committee was established to do this and contributions came from each group. Often an annual budget had to be established for these joint enterprises. The emerging complex was called the women's association. Occasionally, joint luncheons or meetings were held to which all women were invited. A number of churches continue to use this federated plan and find it very satisfactory. Most of the old friction has given place to cordial relations and cooperation. The plan has proven flexible. New organizations have been established as needs have emerged. There is a sense of oneness without loss of old fellowships and specific concerns. The official board of the church has at least one member who also serves on the women's board.

The women's association may become a unified structure, with officers elected by an annual meeting of women, an overall program, and a single budget. All the women of the church may be considered members, or membership may be open to all on the basis of choice and a contribution to the budget. There are committees, or departments, with subcommittees to cover appropriate program areas and activities. Instead of going to a different group for each particular emphasis, every woman is enrolled in one circle or group which has monthly programs developed to deal, over the course of a year, with activities related to all the purposes of the church. Rather than a succession of offerings for the purposes of several organizations, one annual pledge is asked of each woman for the association budget, which usually includes more for the general mission of the church than for local purposes.

Some churches rotate the membership of circles, with an annual drawing of names. This has the advantage of stimulating wide acquaintance. It discourages the development of cliques. It may bring the stimulation of different attitudes and ideas. The most serious disadvantage is the prevention of deep, lasting Christian fellowship which only develops through close association over an extended period. The entire membership is encouraged to attend monthly or quarterly meetings, with programs of general interest. The officers and committee and circle chairmen form an executive board which meets monthly. The president of the association may serve ex officio on the official board, or some of its leaders may be elected to the official board. The association performs invaluable service to the church. It may provide opportunities for Christian growth and usefulness for every sort of woman.

(6) *Men's organizations* may include a men's club and an ushers' association. Sometimes these interests are covered by one organization. The officers are elected at an annual meeting, and there may be monthly meetings for business and programs related to the purposes of the church. There may be committees to cover special interests. There may be small groups for study or work projects.

(7) *Couples groups* should have a minimal organization and no budget. If there are several, an executive committee composed of the chairmen of the groups may perform useful functions. A convenient procedure that avoids many problems is to name each group with a single Greek letter.

c. *Informal organizations* are likely to grow up beside every formal structure. They flourish when strong personalities are left out of the formal structure. When communication is inadequate a luxuriant " grapevine " flourishes. When needs for close fellowship are unmet, " cliques " develop. The remedies for these conditions are obvious, but it is not always possible to apply them. The leaders in a church must therefore be aware of informal structures and plan to use them for the church's purposes. Thus the grapevine may be a second communications system and an exceedingly efficient one. The individual who wants more leadership may not be ready for a board position but may espouse a constructive purpose if given a chance. Healthy group life may be developed with the aid of those about whom people gather naturally.

4. Experiments in Structure

There is widespread concern about whether existing forms of congregational organization help or hinder the purposes of the church. The Third Assembly of the World Council of Churches at New Delhi, troubled by the ineffectiveness of present-day evangelism, called for a study of "The Missionary Structure of the Congregation." The commission which has begun this task suggests that changes in the forms of congregational life may facilitate the development of fellowships better prepared for worship and nurture, as well as witness, in the modern world. So far the attention has been devoted largely to diagnosis. A bibliography issued in February, 1962, lists more than a hundred books by authors as different as Karl Barth and Peter Berger, but the structural changes proposed are few in number.

A great deal more attention ought to be given to this subject by pastors and church members who are working at the local level where new possibilities may take shape. Most of the literature now refers again and again to a limited number of well-known experiments in America, Britain, France, Germany, and India. Program suggestions that emerge from these imaginative efforts will be considered later in this book. The structural innovations that now call for attention may be reduced to four:

a. *Organization along functional lines* is one possibility. Every member is assigned for three years to one of the commissions, and through it to a task in the church or community. There are no other organizations or groups except the official board. Thus a member attends weekly worship and a weekly or monthly meeting of his commission. He may perform most of his service in the church or in a community agency. Commission meetings include periods for study and prayer. There are no divisions by age or sex, except for children of precommunicant age who attend classes for instruction. This arrangement radically cuts down the amount of time devoted by Christians to meetings and the machinery of organization. It emphasizes the obligation of the whole people of God to carry forward the purposes of the church in the world. It is most suitable for a church of modest size.

It has disadvantages. Ability and willingness for vigorous service on the part of every member are assumed. This may be unrealistic. A limited variety of experience is available in any period. The longer relationships that develop into rich fellowship are ruled out by the triennial changes.

b. *Organization based on small personal groups* is a second possibility. There are no other organizations except an official board composed of one representative from each group. A group has eight to twenty members, and may be called a cell, a prayer group, a research group, or a house church. The meetings are held weekly in homes, and include study and prayer and discussion of aspects of the Christian life. Some action projects are undertaken by each group, and each seeks to grow by reaching new persons for Christ. Growing groups divide to form two. There is no division by age or sex, but small groups of youth are established since both adults and young people find it hard to be open in the same group. The only other regular meetings are the weekly common worship in which all the groups come together, and a church school for children. Some plans omit the church school and rely on parents to teach their children. Members of the groups minister to each other, assisted when necessary by the pastor. The pastor's primary tasks are preaching and teaching the group leaders.

This plan conserves some of the energy otherwise devoted to maintaining numerous committees and organizations. It may be started gradually in an old church by the development of some small groups and a policy that lets other organizations wither as they cease to be important. It is more suited to a large congregation than the organization along functional lines. It allows for greater variety of experience and may stimulate more creativity. Variations of the plan are functioning in a number of churches. One weakness lies in the assumption of a high level of spiritual life and commitment on the part of all members, sustained over an indefinite period. A second liability is the necessity for a high percentage of gifted leaders. While Jesus expected a good deal of the apostles, he seems to have made allowances for more limited followers.

c. *Organization based on structures of secular society* is a third possibility. Often this results in a sort of halfway church which does not attempt to carry forward all the purposes of the church, or to elicit full commitment. It is justified on the grounds that the people in established churches are not ready to receive the folks reached by unconventional methods, or those reached are not at home in the ordinary church. This may be due to their limitations or to those of the church. Developments along this line raise questions about the relation of the gospel to the church, and of the church to the Kingdom. They also call for a strategy by which halfway churches become whole or relate their members to churches.

Instances of this type of organization in youth work build on the established relationships in high schools. Personal contacts are first made with recognized leaders among the youth, on the playing fields or in drugstores and other places of assembly. Even after the group starts to meet for Christian reasons, church buildings are avoided and the power structure of the high school is dominant. Sometimes groups are drawn together in a business house or industrial plant. The agent may be a fellow employee who, in some instances, may have a seminary education as well as secular qualifications for his job. Again, professional men or industrial workers may be drawn into groups recruited from particular vocations. Regular meetings may be held for exploration of the gospel in the light of daily experiences. A coffeehouse may be established as a center for persons who may become increasingly serious about knowing Christ and serving him through literature and the arts.

d. *Organization involving a covenanted relation covering every aspect of life* is a fourth possibility. Sometimes a group of this sort shares residential and dining facilities, but in any event they agree in detail to a way of life that includes the same devotional practices, some program of study, and participation in certain projects. They may share all income, or agree to share income until all receive an agreed minimum, or they may commit themselves to be led by a group consensus in the use of income as well as in the employment of time and talent. A group of this sort may establish itself as a colony in a disintegrating neighborhood and attempt a ministry to the people there, drawing them as far into the life of the group as they are willing to come.

Developments in structure are frequently unpremeditated and arise as theological insights affect the efforts of the church to fulfill its mission. The newness may arise from the theology or the situation or the persons involved. It is easier to undertake experiments in new situations where people are not threatened by the possible loss of meaningful relationships. However, a courageous pastor will find an older church ready for adventure after the people become well acquainted with him and know that he appreciates the real values already established in their common life.

CHAPTER V

Recruiting and Training Volunteers

The hardest and most rewarding pastoral task is the development of strong leaders. Our Lord devoted a major portion of his time to this endeavor. He saw possibilities in the most unlikely persons. After a night of prayer he chose twelve men and made their training one of the central motifs of his ministry. He talked with them about the things he considered most important. He visited in their homes. He gave them responsibilities. He demonstrated a style of living, and showed them how to live and work together in love. He trusted them to do things beyond their strength—and they did. He knew that even he could not alone accomplish his mission.

1. A PERSONNEL COMMITTEE

An effective Christian ministry emerges only as a pastor gives primary attention to the recruiting and training of volunteers. But he cannot do this by himself. He must develop a personnel committee. It should be a representative group that meets regularly. In a very small church the official board may perform this function. In a large congregation it may be a committee related to the executive committee or the stewardship commission.

A primary task of the personnel committee is to determine what positions must be filled. This may be determined by a survey that includes inquiries addressed to each board, department, or commission, each committee and organization. A *job analysis* may be worked out for each position. It should outline the work to be done, the relationships involved, the result desired, and the qualities needed for effective performance. Some churches have an *organizational manual* for each board or commission. It states briefly what is expected of all church members, of members of the board, and of committee members.

2. Sources of Volunteers

The pastor and officers, and others who visit or work with members, will be encouraged to create a *favorable climate* for recruiting. This will arise from an awareness of the need felt by each Christian for the expression of faith in action. It will grow as leaders communicate enthusiasm for the work going on in the church and for services members are performing in the community. It will develop alertness to discover people with special gifts and report them to the committee. A *policy of development* may be recommended to nominating committees and appointing officers, so that church workers will be advanced from modest to more demanding tasks.

A *personnel file* may be maintained. This will be the committee's working tool. It will include information about members who are performing services in the church or community, and should be kept up to date. Some churches use *time and talent surveys,* with cards on which members are asked to record past and present activities and current interests. The survey may be initiated with the thorough training of visitors who will call on every member with a card to be filled out. Thereafter, new members will be asked to give the answers on a card at the time they are received. Sometimes all the entries are made by interviewers rather than by the members themselves. This may reduce the tendency of members to be reticent about their abilities, but it will not eliminate this liability of the survey method. A serious danger is the adverse reaction that arises when a person indicates interest in an activity, but is not invited to participate for a long time because there are no vacancies, or through neglect. *Indexing* of the personnel file may be by simple alphabetical name sequence. The next step may be use of colored tabs to denote special abilities. A further possibility is a simple Key-sort file which allows for a large number of classifications. The cards of people with particular abilities may be found by threading a thin rod through marginal holes. A very large church may be able to afford a more versatile punched card system.

Special projects make ideal opportunities for getting acquainted with the abilities of new persons. There should be a definite policy of including at least a substantial percentage of new members in projects such as the Every Member Canvass, evangelistic visitations, and festivals.

3. Invitation, Election, and Installation

The invitation to serve will not ordinarily come from the personnel committee. This group serves as a center of reference for the nominating committee, the Christian education commission, and the other committees and organizations. It may encourage a standardization of procedure.

Visits to prospects for nomination will always be by two persons and there will be no telephone recruiting. The visitors will offer a written description of the job or an organizational manual. Following a discussion, the visitors will, if necessary, offer to call back for an answer. An alternative plan is the offering of invitations at *meetings*. A group of persons is selected and invited by mail, with a telephone follow-up if necessary. The invitation may be for lunch or dinner or an evening at the church to deal with a subject of "great importance." The host will be the chairman of the nominating committee. Officers of the board or commission involved and the pastor may be present. There will be a verbal presentation with written materials, and a few enthusiastic comments from current workers. The chairman will ask the invited candidates to give him their answers privately after the meeting. The advantages of this plan include the certainty of a good presentation, group enthusiasm, and the demonstration of the quality of persons involved. The major disadvantage is that when there are refusals a second group must be invited.

The names of those to be elected by a congregation will be presented to the annual meeting by a *nominating committee*. Denominational law may include provisions for the nomination and election of the members of this committee. If the congregation itself is to make the rules, it may elect a maximum of nine persons, three each year for three-year terms, with no more than two from the official board, and at least three who are not currently serving on a board or commission. Nominations to this committee may be made by the nominating committee or a special committee. Arrangements for the annual meeting of the congregation and for a service of installation may be made by the nominating committee or the personnel committee. Most communions have suggested orders for installations.

4. Training and Evaluation

Group conferences may be held for those newly elected if they were not involved in a meeting before nomination. The pastor and leaders of their boards or organizations may lead discussions concerning their new responsibilities. Personal coaching may be planned for important jobs, with the pastor or a church officer responsible for informal conferences. A church officers training course may be offered annually in the church, or for those from a group of churches under the auspices of the denomination or council of churches. The personnel committee may prepare a small list of books to be made available to those newly elected. The church may adopt a plan for regular presentations at board and commission meetings. Those who are going to teach or visit may observe a veteran at work, and discuss the operation afterward. Each may also work first as a partner of an experienced person.

The personnel committee may wish to make continuous studies of the degree of participation of the membership, and of the performance of those who do accept responsibilities. About one person in five seems to be " allergic " to group activity and should probably be offered other kinds of opportunity for service. A fourth of those who accept places in the organizational life of the church will do little about it after election. This discourages others. The committee may discover why some people are not effective in organizations, and take steps to remedy the situation. Often the problem lies in training plans or inadequate programs. If nothing constructive appears possible, they can at least see that these persons are not advanced to other posts.

Active interest in group activity tends to increase with each year of formal education and to decrease after the fiftieth birthday. This may be due, in part, to the kinds of activity offered by the church and community. The committee may discover new opportunities for fellowship and service attractive to persons with limited education and to older persons.

Chapter VI

Church Employees

Some of the best working conditions in the world and some of the worst are to be found in churches. A sermon dealing with abuses in society is something less than challenging to those who know the sexton receives a starvation wage, and it is grotesquely funny to hear a homily on love from a preacher who is mean to those who work with him. The pastor of one large church was the laughingstock of a business community. Said one company president, " We would not tolerate a foreman who had his turnover in employees." On the other hand, there are churches where every member of the staff is thrilled to be part of a creative effort and the ordinary frictions are unimportant. The difference is largely a matter of spirit, but this cannot be maintained without sound personnel practices. Persons must be well chosen for their tasks and work under competent supervision within clearly defined policies and relationships. The best program will be ineffective without Christian love, but a minister who " just loves people " and " plays it by ear " will soon be surrounded by difficult and frustrated people. Pastors and officers need to think about a number of things in this connection.

1. The Staff Committee

There should be a staff committee responsible for employment policies, job descriptions, recommendations regarding initiation or termination of employment, and the establishment or change of compensation. This group should be aware of the demands of social justice and see that the church is a leader, not a follower, in these matters. It will deal with problems that arise and may review the performance of employees from time to time. The official board may serve as the staff committee in a small church. It may ask its executive committee to perform this function in a larger church. If there is a separate board of trustees or other major board, its officers may be invited to sit with the executive committee when it acts as staff committee. The pastor may preside or be an ex officio member of the committee, except when he is personally involved.

2. Needs

The employees needed will depend on the size of the congregation and the nature of its program. Let us examine four classes of services and the various positions that may be established to meet these needs.

a. *Pastoral Services.* The church's first employee in this area, after the pastor, may be a *seminary student* who will be available on Saturday afternoon and Sunday and will assist with a youth group, make some visits, and take a part in the leadership of worship. The church may prefer to have a *church visitor,* an able woman or retired minister, available five afternoons a week for visiting and possibly at other times for supervision of volunteer visitors. It may, instead, wish to use a *children's work supervisor* or *a youth adviser.* These persons may be public-school teachers available Sundays and one or two evenings to recruit and instruct teachers, supervise or advise in the area of their responsibilities. The church's choice of helpers should depend upon the pastor's strengths and weaknesses, the demands of the program, and the persons available.

In a somewhat larger church, the employee may be an *assistant in Christian education,* usually a young woman who prepared for this task in college. If there are more adequate resources, there may be a *director of Christian education,* usually a man or woman who received an M.R.E. degree after two years of seminary work.

The next step may be another minister who will carry responsibility in one or several program areas. Usually, an additional minister is called and installed as assistant pastor and is made an associate pastor after one or two years of mutual satisfaction. A man of proven ability may join the staff as associate pastor. These titles describe an official relation to the church and in many cases are used only in official papers.

When he is to work primarily in one area this man may be called minister of education, minister to youth, administrative minister, minister of evangelism, or minister of visitation. Often the title corresponds to the name of the official board's department or commission. A designation of this sort may help to make him more acceptable to church members who will think of him as performing a task for which he was called, not merely assisting the minister in this. A visit from the minister of visitation is not so likely to leave the parishioner feeling that *the* minister has not called but has sent an assistant. Some churches, on the other hand, feel that whatever his rank or function each minister of the church should be simply listed as one of the pastors of the church. When the senior pastor shares this view it does not take very long before each man is accepted in terms of the functions he can best perform. As in the case of physicians, ministers who work together in this way discover that some persons and families relate more readily to different ministers and their united service is stronger and more helpful to the whole people than the single ministry of any one of them could be.

A few churches have decided to eliminate even the official differences and have installed several men as pastors, expecting that executive authority and supervision will be rotated or shared. Except in cases where one of the group is actually recognized as the leader because of his preeminent gifts, this does not seem to work out very well in the long run. In a staff of any size which has organizational responsibilities, there must be a continuing executive officer. The alternatives are cumbersome and time-consuming arrangements or conflict.

It is a curious fact that the local church is the only institution in which anyone thinks of proposing a staff arrangement without authority relationships. No one would suggest it for a seminary or college or church board. The reason seems to be that men attracted to the ministry tend to be individualists. They generally prefer roles such as preaching and counseling, in which they are on their own, to roles such as administration, in which they are working with other people in a team relationship. The freewheeling way of life cherished by some ministers is a luxury denied to most of their neighbors. It appears as an anachronism in larger churches in which there must be a number of full-time workers. Perhaps we need to introduce experiences in the process by which ministers are trained for their tasks which will make it clear that subordination in an administrative pattern has little to do with the relative importance of the task performed. It may also be important to develop an awareness that in a joint enterprise persons of varying ability and experience should expect to work at different levels of responsibility and authority.

The other side of the coin is that congregations and senior pastors must learn to be more generous in sharing appreciation and income with staff members. After minimum needs of the families involved are met, it is reasonable to have salary variations based on the relative value of contributions, but this rarely justifies one salary three times that of the next staff member on the scale.

A minister should have seminary-trained associates only if he is secure enough to give them full scope for growth and to welcome their successes. When another minister's preaching is enthusiastically received, or when the other seems more popular with some groups, the senior pastor must come to terms with any threat he feels, or decide to use only lay associates. Some very effective ministers have inferiority problems which would yield only to such heroic therapy that it is wiser for them to serve churches which can get along with one minister and part-time helpers. The alternative is usually unconscious choice of weak associates who, by their ineffectual performance, increase the minister's problems.

All the positions listed under " Pastoral Services " may exist in a very large church. The generally accepted rule is one full-time pastoral worker, or his equivalent, for every six hundred members, though this may be inadequate when there is an active program. Three part-time workers may do more than a full-time person, at less expense. This is particularly true when the needed services must be performed within a limited period, as on Sunday mornings or evenings, or during the three afternoon hours and two evening hours when most visiting must occur.

A church may decide to use as assistants men just graduated

from seminary. Men of outstanding ability may be available at this point in their careers and can make a fine contribution to the church during the three years they are likely to stay. However, the church and pastor accept an obligation to prepare such talented young men for effective ministries. This is time-consuming and requires a willingness to put up with mistakes and take risks.

Seminary interns who come to the church for a year between their second and third years in school need the experience and can bring much to a congregation. This is an expensive form of help in terms of staff time, however. It should be undertaken only when a church understands and is willing to consider part of the salary as support of theological education. The intern's contribution is likely to go only a little beyond compensating for time the minister and staff devote to him. Only multiple-staff churches are well prepared for this service.

b. *Supporting Services.* Such services come from those persons equipped to help with areas in which the church's activities parallel those of the business world. A good secretary may release as much as a third of a minister's time for his primary tasks. Except under unusual circumstances, the first employee after the minister, the organist, and the sexton, should be a part-time secretary, and then a full-time secretary. Most churches of more than three hundred members can afford this, and it is a sound use of money.

In larger churches the tasks may be apportioned to a church secretary, a pastor's secretary, and a financial secretary. Sometimes the work of the church and financial secretaries is assigned to a business manager who has responsibility for records, stewardship, finances, the use of building and equipment, and purchasing. A receptionist may greet visitors, handle incoming telephone calls, and do some typing and routine operations for staff members. Volunteers may undertake this responsibility on a regular schedule.

c. *Music.* The organist will be the first employee with musical responsibilities, and except in the largest churches this will be a part-time position. Choral direction may be a task of the organist or there may be a separate choir director, who will then be responsible to the official board for the musical program. There are some musicians who have also earned seminary degrees and may be installed in large churches as full-time ministers of music. Sometimes it is wise to have separate choral directors for age-group choirs, under the guidance of the choir director or minister of music. Several paid soloists may be very helpful to the director in the development of an effective church choir.

d. *Housekeeping Services.* The sexton is an important worker. Feelings about the church, developed by members and strangers, will be affected by his attitude and the quality of his work. This should be kept in mind when he and his helpers are employed. The church may employ a custodian to assist the sexton. Sometimes a housekeeper or maid is employed to care for parlors and kitchens and bathrooms. A hostess or caterer may prepare meals and arrange for receptions or assist women's association committees in these enterprises. This person may be on a salary and supervise part-time kitchen and dining room employees, or may supply catering service on the basis of agreed charges per meal.

3. Selection

a. *Sources.* Ministers and other pastoral workers may be found through the denominations' personnel offices, seminary alumni offices, and recommendations from individuals. Candidates for other positions may be discovered through advertisements in classified sections of newspapers, suggestions from interested persons, placement offices of business schools, and employment agencies. For most positions, it is wise to seek individuals dedicated to the church's purposes, but not members of the church they will serve. This protects the congregation against internal strife if the employee proves to be inadequate. In this connection, it is best to use a box number, rather than the church address, in advertising positions.

b. *References.* References should be secured for every potential employee, and should come from individuals not related to the prospect nor interested in his or her relocation. The subject of the inquiry has a right to protection in this process; if he has not suggested the reference, it should be made clear that the inquirer does not know the person named to be interested in the position. References also deserve protection and their replies should be destroyed after a decision is made. Some churches are shockingly careless about such things. Specific questions should be asked in letters to references: "Please comment on his preaching, his pastoral work, his administrative capacity." "Does he relate well to people?" If these questions are not answered, there should be a follow-up by telephone. People will say things that they will not write.

c. *Interviews.* Interviews with candidates for a position require preparation. The interviewer will have a statistical knowledge of the prospect and some information from references. He will be familiar with the job description of the position to be filled. There will be a list of things he needs to know in order to decide whether this person can do the job: health and appearance, character and dedication to the purposes of the church, education and experience, required skills and ability to work with other people. He will wish to explore family background and present home life, work record and spare-time activities, as these things will affect performance.

The *structure* of the interview should not be rigid, but there ought to be a plan. The interviewer will determine where he wishes to begin and the kinds of things he will know when the exchange is over. He will have in mind some possible topics for initiating the conversation, and questions which will keep it moving toward his goals. An open and friendly *atmosphere* will make it easier for the applicant to express himself. The interviewer should give his visitor complete attention, having arranged in advance for an absolute minimum of interruption. He will plan to talk as little as possible after his opening statement.

The *nature of the work* to be done and the interviewer's feeling about its importance should be communicated at the outset. Brevity is a virtue in this connection, but even more important is an accurate picture of the job and of the style of life shared by workers in the church. Some applicants will visibly lose interest at this point, and time will be saved by everyone. Making this presentation at the beginning is much fairer to the potential worker. This is especially true when three or four persons are to be interviewed before a decision is made and an enthusiastic picture of the position at the end of an interview may create the false impression that a choice has been made. Properly done, this presentation will also set the stage for openness on the part of the applicant.

Questions are used primarily to keep the prospect talking, and sometimes a long pause may be more effective. Questions may be necessary to get the session going, to secure more information or fill in a gap in the story. It may occasionally be helpful to rephrase a statement to be sure it has been understood. Questions are of little value if they suggest their own replies or require " yes " or " no " answers.

In the *interpretation* of the interview, it is essential to discount one's own biases and prejudices, to weigh the effects of superficial impressions, to avoid conclusions based on one success or one failure. The important factors are character and knowledge or skill, interest in people and the ability to work with them. If one's impressions differ from the implications of references, there should be a further check before decision.

4. Staff Relationships

Persons are employed by a church to get things done. It is essential that their relationships facilitate this purpose.

a. *Job Descriptions.* If this is to be the case, each person must know what he is to do and how this is related to what others are doing. A written job description will be valuable in this connection. If the position is new, the first attempt to describe it may be inadequate, but it can be improved through consultation and correction. Continuing positions should be formally redefined from time to time as experience suggests changes. A job description will list the things to be done, the authority that goes with these responsibilities, and the necessary relationships.

b. *Executive Authority.* Experience indicates that some form of executive authority is essential if there is to be coordination and effective performance. The pastor, or the senior pastor if there are several ministers, is usually charged by the church officers to exercise executive authority over the other employees. He convenes the staff and makes executive decisions in areas in which no one is specifically charged with authority. He meets with the staff committee in consideration of all employment except his own. He also provides supervision of those working in the area of pastoral services.

His authority may have limits specified in his job description and those of other employees. Decisions about the music staff will usually be in the hands of the official board's music committee, and the minister of music or choir director will have executive authority and responsibility for supervision. Housekeeping services will frequently be under the guidance of the official board's property commission, with the sexton expected to supervise other employees. When there is a business manager, he usually has executive authority and supervisory responsibility for employees in supporting services and housekeeping services, working under the guidance of the pastor, the staff committee, and the building committee, according to specifications in his job description.

When there are several persons in pastoral services, each may have authority for coordinating the work of the others in the area of his specialization. Thus, the minister or church visitor charged with pastoral care makes all visiting assignments for both staff and volunteers. The other ministers and staff members visit, as assigned, and clear all calls in advance with the person in charge. The minister or director of Christian education makes all assignments in this area, which will include youth activity, unless there is a minister or director of youth activities. The minister responsible for worship plans the services and assigns responsibilities for participation.

All these tasks are simplified by the adoption of policies which may, in the course of time, be written into job descriptions. Thus it may be understood that the minister responsible for worship will usually preach and that the others will take some part in the service when available, and will preach on specified occasions or a certain number of times. The conduct of Baptisms, weddings, and funerals may be the responsibility of the person asked, which is frequently a happy arrangement, or may be assigned by either the minister responsible for worship or the person responsible for pastoral care.

Each worker in pastoral services may work directly with one or more departments or commissions of the official board. Meeting with a department or commission, he will help in working out plans and projects and developing leaders. A worker in a smoothly functioning staff group will wish to discuss with the whole staff proposals he intends to offer his department and to report on departmental problems, discussions, and plans.

c. *Staff Meetings*. If a church staff is to work together, there must be regular meetings. In many churches there is a brief chapel service at the beginning of each day. The order may come from a denominational prayer book or follow a devotional guide such as *Today* or *The Upper Room*. Each staff member who is willing may take a turn in the leadership. Frequently, there is intercession for families in the church. This may be based on a plan that includes a certain number each day, with special places made for a shut-in or two and for those bereaved or seriously ill.

Usually there is a brief meeting of the whole staff early in the week, with a quick review of last week's activities and those projected for the current week to be sure there are no loose ends. Then the schedule for next week is presented and approved for publication. Each person is given an opportunity to present any special concerns. Failure to offer this opening in a way that encourages participation can lead to feelings of frustration or the conclusion that some tasks are considered unimportant. Some large staff groups have each member bring a brief written report on last week's major activities. These are passed around at the meeting so that all are aware of the extent of the others' labors.

Following this general staff meeting, which may last from fifteen minutes to an hour, the pastoral services staff may continue in session or convene later to consider programs, projects, and leaders, arrange assignments, and report to each other. At this meeting the person responsible for visitation will distribute cards for visits and receive written reports on calls which may be discussed. Usually, this meeting can be concluded in less than an hour, though there may be occasions when longer periods are justifiable, and there ought to be at least one daylong conference before the congregational planning process gets under way late in the spring.

d. *Supervision.* The task of the supervisor is so to appraise the performance of the worker that the worker grows in the ability to appraise his own performance and may, therefore, improve it. Broad experience indicates that every worker may profit from periodic consultations about his performance.

This may proceed at one of two levels. The supervisor may assign tasks and check on the proper fulfillment of the assignments, or he may delegate responsibility for certain results and consult later on what happened. A pastor may tell the sexton to set up six tables and fifty chairs arranged in a U formation in the Blue Room by nine A.M. on Friday, and he may be there at nine A.M. to see that it has been done. He may prefer instead to reach agreement with the sexton that there will be adequate preparation for each of the groups listed on the monthly schedule. When they sit down for evaluation, he will expect to discuss the adequacy of arrangements for a month or more, and will hope for suggestions from the sexton for improving the way things are done.

One senior minister gives each of his associates detailed instructions about every project week by week and is constantly checking to see that co-workers do as he directs. Another blocks out areas of responsibility when a new staff member arrives. They reach agreement about results that may be expected. The new man learns how much authority he has and how he is to relate to other staff members. This discussion takes place in connection with a written job description approved by the staff committee, which the two men revise for further committee consideration and approval. Each retains a copy of the accepted description.

The next conference is held a month later. The newcomer's performance is compared with their mutual expectations as recorded in the job description. They agree on revisions suggested by opportunities or difficulties in the situation or by special abilities or limitations in the worker himself. He arranges to meet some of the inadequacies, which have become apparent, by reading or securing needed training or charting new courses of action. One young minister asked at the time of this interview for regular weekly conferences for discussion and criticism of prayers he prepared for public worship. Another requested extra leave of half a day a week for some clinical training at a nearby hospital. A youth worker planned to undertake a university extension course in the evenings. A secretarial worker decided to change the pattern of her spare-time activity. On the other hand, there have been occasions when a whole program has been scrapped, as beyond the resources of the staff, or a completely new possibility has emerged. The important factor in these interviews is reality. The senior pastor tries to be objective and encourages staff members to be open with him about his own limitations and the imperfections of the program, but he does not allow them in this way to escape self-appraisal and the adoption of definite measures for growth. The job description is altered at the end of the interview in terms of new mutual expectations.

Appraisal conferences follow at six months' intervals for the first two years, then come annually. The mere existence of a supervisory plan encourages the church staff in objective self-appraisal, without which the finest motivation may end in wasted motion. In order to complete the process, the pastor asks a member of the staff committee to help him review his progress annually.

A third pastor has a different approach. He maps out large areas of authority and responsibility for each of his associates and makes no attempt at formal supervision. Indeed, a visitor at a staff meeting may get the impression that sovereign individuals are consulting each other for help as they carry forward tasks beyond their capacity. The senior pastor often invites more assistance from the others than they do from him, but a keen visitor will soon observe who gives staff members the confidence to attempt things beyond their apparent capacities and experience; who raises the right questions; and who insists on realistic appraisal of efforts and results. This man has developed some remarkable associates, but his method is more difficult than it looks. It should be attempted only by a person skilled in more direct supervision, who is able to be enthusiastic about gifts – lacking in him – which are to be found in his associates. It is not to be confused with the abdication of supervisory responsibility by which some pastors attempt to escape all involvement in aspects of the ministry distasteful to them.

Chapter VII

Working with Groups

Life in the church is life together. Persons responding to God's love in Christ come to him and immediately find themselves in company with others drawn to him. The gathering may involve persons of very different backgrounds, interests, and abilities. This was true of the original disciples. The circle around Jesus included rich and poor, educated and ignorant, patriot and quisling. Where the church is alive and responsive to its Lord, this same explosive mixture of persons is likely to be found in many small groups through which it performs its functions of worship, nurture, and witness.

His Spirit creates these groups and makes their continued existence possible. Divine grace brings them together and enables them to live together in love. The union in the church of people who would otherwise have nothing in common is a daily miracle that goes beyond nature by grace. But grace does not suspend all human emotions, nor change all the elements in group behavior. There is ample evidence that persons in a company of Christians react to one another most of the time very much as others do. The power of Christian love has entered on the side of the centripetal forces at work in the group, but all the forces moving toward the center as well as all the centrifugal forces must be taken into account.

1. Group Dynamics

Those persons charged with the task of pastoral administration will do well to be aware of the new information emerging from the study of group dynamics. In every group there are two levels of activity. There is the level of ideas, sometimes called the task area. This is the sphere in which members try to communicate with one another for the purpose of solving the problems or performing the tasks for which the group has come together. The secondary level is often unnoticed. Activities in this sphere are sometimes described as the hidden agenda. This does not refer to a secret plan by which some intend to manipulate others. It describes, rather, emotional engagements below the level of consciousness in which members seek to feel one another out, and maneuver in order to establish the kind of interpersonal relationships which make them comfortable and happy.

This undercover struggle can make it impossible for a group to perform effectively at the task level. The purpose of the group may be less important to its members than their own desires for security, recognition, status, or power. When a pastor has an unnoticed " necessity " to prove his importance by dominating an official board or a staff, there will be a strong unconscious tendency on the part of the board or staff members to defend their integrity by opposing his proposals at the idea level. When a board has a number of insecure members, it will be very hard to secure agreement to a change, however rational it appears. When a person suffers a crushing defeat in a group decision, he may be very polite and " sportsmanlike " about it, but appear unaccountably stubborn on an unrelated issue weeks later. A leader who, in these situations, has his eye only on the group's task level, will find some actions incomprehensible. If, on the other hand, it is possible to plan meetings so that there is emotional satisfaction for all, the main business can be accomplished. When emotions are disregarded because a group is too large or the leader is insensitive, there will usually be smaller groups forming at a corner drugstore or in cars on the way home. Grievances and hurt feelings will be expressed directly or by small criticisms, and people who could not get approval from the large assembly will seek it from a few.

It is obvious that one must function at two levels in working with groups. At the thought level there will be a concern to effect real communication between members of the group. It may be helpful to ask a person to restate an opponent's position to his satisfaction before pressing objections. The leader will also be at some pains to prevent the group from confusing disagreement with hostility. Where some of the problem appears to arise from a fault in logic, it may be possible to restate a position in such a way that the proponent may correct the logic without losing face. When two opposing views have much in common, it may be fruitful to rephrase each in such a way that the important agreements may be seen and accepted. Then the group can move on to deal with remaining issues in a process that repeats this cycle.

Group work at the task level may be facilitated if there is a capable recorder to note and review points of agreement. Another person may be appointed to watch the clock after a time budget (docket) has been approved for the meeting. The presiding officer must keep the members from getting lost in excursions, and should try to clarify propositions by restatements, questions, and summaries. He will also try to give opportunity and develop a congenial atmosphere for new ideas.

At the level of interpersonal relations, the leader needs to become aware of the dynamic nature of the group. He will find centers of influence and dependents, patterns of friendship and hostility. A new practice called "sociometry" charts group relationships. Persons in a group may be asked to return confidential questionnaires dealing with their relationships. Little circles representing persons are linked with arrows to show patterns of status, dependency, or friendship. In another approach, the diagram is drawn by an observer to plot the course of a group conversation. An arrow or arrows are drawn from circle to circle each time a member addresses one or several others. Everyone may be invited to view the illuminating result at the end of the meeting. A third procedure is to secure unsigned reactions at the end of a meeting to questions about the degree of satisfaction with the meeting and its procedures. These sociometric practices are particularly applicable to small groups studying the problems of leadership. One who has thus been made aware of the unseen currents in a meeting will be a more adequate teacher or moderator.

"Sensitivity courses" are given under American Management Association auspices as well as by universities and group dynamics study centers. One method in much use is to place a group of people in a room for a long period without a chairman or docket. As one after another attempts to assume leadership and is thwarted by others, the group becomes very much aware of the jungle of emotions on the hidden agenda. They also see that relationships and positions once established are thereafter protected by social pressure. It is also apparent that when enough members become dissatisfied with a prevailing structure, a seemingly insignificant act or word may bring about change. Some persons seem to sense instinctively the presence of hidden crosscurrents in a group. They move through them as a sailor tacks against contrary winds. Most of us, however, will profit from the emerging insights of group dynamics.

Atmosphere in a meeting is important. This includes physical arrangements that provide comfort and avoid placing persons in dominating positions. The ideal is a circle or a square table with an equal number on each of four sides. While crowding is to be avoided, it has been definitely established that the greater the distance between persons in a face-to-face group the more likely they are to disagree. The use of a table with a large name card in front of each person makes it easier for everyone to respond on a personal basis and it provides an opportunity for the chairman to distribute talkative persons around the circle and to keep factions from lining up on two sides of a table or room.

The psychological climate will be affected by these physical arrangements, and by the attitudes and acts of the leader. If he is sincerely interested in each person and shows respect and understanding, these attitudes are likely to prevail. If he welcomes expressions of opinion contrary to his own, the group will soon learn to be free and open. If he guides proceedings so that everyone is drawn into the discussion and overaggressive participants are controlled, a pattern of fair play will soon be appreciated and protected by all. When a leader has to deal with a very aggressive effort by one member who is trying to manipulate and control the group, it may be necessary to let his behavior continue to the point that the motivation is obvious. At this point group pressures will come into play. Sometimes the problem can be solved by offering responsibility, or eliciting help with the unresponsive.

The opening of a meeting can be a critical period. It is not by accident that diplomatic gatherings often begin with a good dinner. Persons who have learned to enjoy one another's company are much less inclined to tear at one another even when they disagree. Time is not wasted in which a leader invites introductions, or talks in such a way as to make everyone feel comfortable and friendly and relaxed.

Sometimes, of course, it is known that there are strong feelings on two sides of an issue and that personal feelings of importance or security are attached to the success or failure of a proposition or a project. In this case the leader may encourage, at the outset, expressions of strong feeling. Under this type of leadership the first half of a first meeting may seem to be moving away from any hope of solution. As a matter of fact, when the violent emotion has been spent, the more rational natures of the members will begin to assert themselves and deal constructively with the issue. However, a novice should not attempt this approach unless he is sure he will stay cool himself, and that the group will not polarize into two groups. At the beginning there should be quiet restatement of feelings, making the feeling element apparent. Later, as thoughts begin to be more important, they may be harmonized.

There are occasions when feelings are required as allies of a constructive approach to the tasks of the group. In this circumstance, the leader's obligation is to encourage emotional involvement. This may be true when an official board is considering sponsorship of a refugee family. If they feel the anxieties engendered by obvious problems more than the unfortunate plight of the family, they will not undertake the responsibility. All the board members may be involved by presentation of a letter from the family, a film or filmstrip about the plight of refugees, a vivid account of the gratitude of another family under care of a neighboring church, or by a personal visit from a refugee. When a board or committee is considering a case of youthful vandalism in the church building, or the establishment of a community youth program, or the opening of a storefront mission, a mimeographed case study read by all and then discussed may lead to deep concern and action.

Another possibility in situations of this sort is role-playing, in which members of the group take the parts of persons they wish to understand. They are assigned their parts and given the outlines of a dramatic situation which they are to act out before the others. In each instance they are to assume the personality of the part they play. Role-playing (also called psychodrama or sociodrama) may be effective in any situation where it is important for one person to understand another's feelings. Young people's groups have been led to new attitudes toward parents through role-playing, and groups of parents have been led to new insights. Reluctance to deal creatively with housing problems has yielded to the involvement produced by role-playing.

2. Resolving Conflict

New Testament narratives and experience in church and family make it plain that love does not prevent conflict, though it makes it less threatening to the persons involved. From the beginning, church members have recognized that there may be two ways of dealing with conflict.

a. One way is to order the struggle in ways that will be of least harm to all concerned and will result in a clear-cut victory for one point of view. The parties may be called upon to present their views to an authority or court of the church. Once a decision is given, the argument is over. Another procedure for orderly conflict is that which provides debate on an issue under parliamentary law, ending in a binding decision by majority vote. When struggle is the only way to resolve disagreement, the pastoral administrator has an obligation to see that the laws are enforced with equity and that cases are fairly presented. Minority rights must be protected with allowance of adequate time and opportunity to win others to the minority view. Once a decision is reached, it must be accepted by all or the dissidents must withdraw.

It must be noted that a legal battle before a church court or a parliamentary struggle for a majority vote may be enjoyed by a good many of the participants as it offers a socially acceptable and usually harmless way to express aggressive feelings and clear the air. Contenders used to this sort of conflict will often be the best of friends after the question is decided. It is of the utmost importance that nonviolent " fighting " be possible. Where no provision is made for it, and reliance is placed upon Christian love operating without rules, the result is not peace but bitter trouble, as the Corinthians discovered. We may be thankful for our carefully articulated books of order and discipline.

b. However, the second way of dealing with conflict is usually preferable, if it is possible. This is the way of integration, which arrives at an agreement that incorporates the thinking of the whole group.

The leader's function in this process is to help the company to reach a consensus. At the task level this involves efforts to be sure there is adequate communication so that each person understands the meaning of statements by others. The group is entitled to all the available information on the subject under discussion, including established facts, expert opinion, and historical precedents. Sound reasoning should be safeguarded by questions that expose false logic. Differences in values may be reconciled by discussion of the style of life found in Jesus Christ.

If there is to be a reconciliation of views, the leader must be sensitive to all that happens at the emotional level. Statements bristling with hostility may be drained of emotion by restatement or by use of light humor. Heavily charged issues may be delayed until agreement has been reached on other points. When antagonists lock horns the leader may introduce another matter, draw others into the discussion, or shift the lines of battle by suggesting that both may be wrong! Tension may sometimes be dissipated by a coffee break or recess. When the tide begins to run toward a consensus, the sensitive leader eases the way of those who must yield at some points by emphasizing their positive contributions. He expresses the group's satisfaction in reaching harmony so that there will be little temptation for anyone to gloat. It will be noted that all we learn about the obstructive power of unfortunate emotions underlines the importance for group activity of the love engendered by the sacrifice of Christ and by the power of his Spirit. The best techniques will not result in effective Christian groups unless the members have some measure of this love.

3. Effecting Change

a. Change is needed in a congregation or church group when dominant purposes have no sound relation to the church's reason for existence. Thus, a congregation may be devoting all its energies to the development of elaborate buildings or to gathering into its membership a social elite. A church organization may be interested in perpetuating itself at any cost, or all its meetings may be focused on an annual bazaar. Change is also needed when organizations or activities do not serve the church's purposes of worship, nurture, and witness. This may be due to a faulty structure that concentrates power in a few hands, or allows for inadequate communication between groups, or ties up too much energy in elaborate machinery or unnecessary activity. It may result from ineffective leadership not endowed with necessary intelligence, adaptability, or skill. It may involve a poor deployment of resources, arising from insensitivity to the church's environment.

b. Forces favorable to change include dissatisfaction with the present situation. This may be due to perception of a gap between the actual and the ideal in the realm of purpose or performance. It may flow from feelings of concern for neglected persons, annoyance at overdominant leaders, frustration at waste caused by an inefficient structure, or discouragement with progress toward a goal. A desire for change may be heightened by knowledge of the benefits it has conferred on another group, or of the dissolution or disaster fallen upon a comparable group that did not change. Change is encouraged, once it has begun, by the human need to complete a task in which there has been an investment of time or money.

c. Forces resistant to change include convictions that the present goals are sound or the arrangements adequate. Sometimes it may be thought that differences would be an improvement but that the group cannot effect or sustain them due to inadequate time or money or energy, or because of a lack of leadership or skill. The strongest resistance usually arises from those persons who feel threatened by proposed changes. They may be insecure persons who are upset by any difference in established patterns. Even a small variation makes them angry. They are furious over the introduction of newer forms of music, or a difference in the order of worship, or the moving of a picture. The church seems to them an island of stability and they resent any change that may occur within it. The pastor should see in their violent reactions invitations to help them find in Christ a security not so easily disturbed.

Objections also come from those persons whose positions or privileges are threatened by change. They may be joined by others who cannot imagine a new state of affairs that will be as satisfactory to them as the present arrangements. Unless persons in this group can be persuaded to look beyond themselves, there will be serious difficulties accompanying efforts to change.

d. Steps toward change include the establishment of the need for it. Information may be obtained by surveys and questionnaires. The experience of other church groups may be studied. The entire group may be involved in analysis of the present situation, through answering questions and studying the data that emerge. The need will be established only when most of the group comes to believe that something better can and should be developed, and that the new state of affairs will bring values more important than the ones that may be lost. This means that alternatives to the present situation must be devised and evaluated. A clear and detailed proposal should emerge and be set forth together with a realistic statement of its advantages and limitations.

Those interested in effecting change must find ways to reinforce the strongest motives favorable to the effort. One of these may turn out to be the lever needed to get things moving. Rational objections deserve fair treatment, and resistant feelings ought to be dealt with creatively. The anxiety that most people feel about change may be somewhat allayed by experience of the new orientation or behavior in a favorable environment. Thus, a church group may spend several days together at a conference center. During this period they may decide to adopt a new purpose and then make all their plans in its light. By the end of the conference they have lived with the novel goal long enough so that it does not seem strange. The same process can make a group feel secure about a new way of doing things. If this feeling is to be conveyed to members who have not attended, the conference must include a representative selection of the membership. Attempts to aid the change process through a conference involving only one member of each group to be affected are likely to have very little effect. Instead of holding a conference the group may prefer to have successive delegations visit a church where the change under consideration has taken place, or they may agree to try the new purpose or arrangement for a limited period.

Plans for change should be so devised that there is public commitment at the time of decision and a likelihood of some early experience of success. Once motion has begun, inertia changes to momentum and everyone who has helped with the process wants his investment to be effective. The change effort will move forward more easily if the reason for it and its goals are understood and accepted, not only by the group involved but also by related groups. Communication is, therefore, very important. Articles in a weekly newsletter and constant interpretation by pastor and officers may be crucial when change is going on within a church. It may also be important to gather the persons affected for discussion as they feel the impact of necessary sacrifices or new demands. Talk of problems may strengthen resolution and help in the development of mutual support. Fruits of change may be celebrated. Appreciation of the effort may appear in sermons and publications. Deputations may be formed to tell other church groups of values served. The process of telling about a new day magnifies its advantages, and wide recognition helps to cement the change.

PART TWO

PROGRAM

Chapter VIII

Worship

The people who risked their lives and climbed over smoking rubble to get into London's churches during the worst of World War II were responding to the love of God in Christ as Christians have done all through the ages. Despite the edicts of Roman emperors and exposure to inhuman tortures, the early Christians came together for worship, and we hear of the same determination among Baptists meeting on back streets in Russia today. Worship is and always will be one of the major activities of the Christian church. It is, of course, inextricably mingled with nurture and witness, but we can isolate these aspects of the Christian response enough to plan for each of them.

1. Preaching

Preaching of the Word of God is one of the essential functions of the church, and it holds a central place in worship. If this is to be well done, some among us must devote a major portion of time to the ministry of the Word. This is a very important obligation for the pastor. An annual preaching plan within a lifetime program makes for the best use of the hours devoted to sermon preparation, ensures a balanced diet for the congregation, and steady growth of the preacher.

A lifetime program may be worked out and reworked year by year in the more leisurely summer months. It will look toward preaching on texts from every part of Scripture and covering all the major subjects of Christian thought and action. It will seek a proper emphasis on important things, without the temptation to ride favorite hobbies. Three work sheets may be useful. One will list the years and show the Bible books from which texts were taken for each season. A second will list the Bible books and show by check marks after them how often in a ministry texts have been chosen from each book. A third will list the major subjects and show by check marks how often they have been treated. This list may be compiled from the index of a theology text or survey, a topical Bible or religious encyclopedia, and the pastor's imagination, and may grow with the years.

An annual preaching plan has its inception as the minister takes a few days in May or June to look ahead. He may work at home or in a seminary library. He will begin with a backward look over the preaching of recent years to see whether there have been important omissions. He will wish to relate his plans to his study program. He will decide to explore the possibilities of certain Bible books and of themes running through the Bible. He may feel the urgency of developing a succession of topics. On the basis of these early inclinations he will begin surveying particular books of the Bible, reading commentaries, and studying chosen subjects, all with a homiletical eye.

One day toward the end of June, using the outline for the coming year which has been worked out in congregational planning sessions, he may prepare, but not fill in, a preaching schedule. Sunday dates for the year will run down the left margin. Following each date there will be space for noting any special emphasis such as Worldwide Communion or Stewardship Sunday. Then there will be space for a sermon topic and text, a Scripture lesson, and the numbers of suggested hymns. Dark horizontal lines may be used to divide the Sundays into seven periods: September, Fall, Advent, Winter, Lent, Spring, and Summer.

Now he will start to think about using certain Bible books or themes for one or the other of these periods. If he has been developing sermon ideas, he should have several hundred texts that cry out for treatment. He must now choose the most urgent, keeping in mind special emphases for particular Sundays and things that will be going on in the church and the world. If possible, he will then work out tentative topics to go with the texts – and this means development of the basic idea. The preaching schedule may be filled in, and made available to the choirmaster so that he may work out his musical program for the year. By this time it is probably early fall. The preaching schedule is confidential and subject to change. It is released for use in publicity one week at a time, about two weeks in advance.

Each of the chosen texts, with its topic, Scripture, and date, may be placed on an 8½″ x 11″ sheet and filed chronologically in a folder. The whole folder is reviewed periodically. The fruits of reading and observation are noted. Relevant clippings are attached to the back of the sheet. Three weeks before it is to be used, the available material is surveyed and considered in the light of the immediate situation. Once in a long while a major change is necessary. Usually the topic is ready for release, and notes are made concerning additional material to be sought. Often one is amazed at the timeliness of the subject chosen months before under the leading of the Holy Spirit.

In the second week before delivery, several outline forms are tried out until the one that seems to fit the subject and material is found. Some preachers give small attention to outlines, with the result that they constantly use the same form or preach sermons largely formless. In the final week the sermon is written, then outlined from the written material and reshaped as necessary to achieve clarity and thrust. One who does not outline again after writing often preaches a sermon without discernible shape or meaning. The preaching outline may be subject to minor changes up to and during the delivery.

2. The Sacraments

The Sacraments involve acts of God through the church. For the sake of good order, while the whole church takes part, the pastor is designated to officiate.

Communion services are being held more frequently. The weekly service of Communion on Sunday mornings, at eight or eight thirty, is a frequent development in churches that have ordinarily held quarterly or monthly Communion. There is little doubt that the early Christians observed the Lord's Supper weekly, and one complaint of some Reformers against Rome was that the people were receiving Communion only a few times a year! There is a good deal of talk about restoring Communion as the main service of worship every Sunday, but this has been done in only a few denominations. Some fear the sermon would tend to deteriorate under this arrangement, some that people would become too casual about Communion, some that the service would be less attractive to outsiders, some that it would be too long! It appears that considerations of expediency are prevailing over the theological ones. There is an increasing use of Communion services in connection with small groups and retreats. The house church idea, with its celebration of the Lord's Supper around a dining table for groups gathered in homes, has proven helpful in a number of situations, though it is not a substitute for the service involving a whole congregation.

The Lord's Supper may be administered at a bedside as a church service. Some denominations make it clear that the church is present by expecting the minister to be accompanied at such times by elders. Many pastors schedule "home Communions" for the sick and shut-ins on the afternoon following celebration of the Lord's Supper at church. Those wishing to be included are invited to send word to the church on a reply card or to telephone the week before. It is noticeable that Communion attendance grows in those churches which take it seriously enough to offer it regularly to those who cannot attend.

Where a group of officers is involved in conduct of a Communion service, careful preparation is essential. If a large number is expected, diagrams of positions and a rehearsal will help. The purpose is to avoid anything that calls attention to the mechanics of the service.

Baptism of adults usually takes place at a public service on a designated Sunday of each month. Infants may be baptized or dedicated at the same service or on the following Sunday. When children are born, the mother is usually in the hospital only a short time and if the baby rooms in with her, the pastor may not be a welcome visitor. Often the most that he can offer is a word of congratulation from the doorway. The first few days at home may not be the best time for a call either, and the pastor may be wise to offer his initial greeting by telephone, then arrange for a convenient visit when he will discuss what is involved in Christian parenthood, and suggest literature. He may be followed by women from a group trained to enroll the parents in preparatory sessions and make arrangements for the Baptism or dedication.

3. Liturgical Leadership

Pastors are commissioned to conduct services of worship primarily because it must be done by someone who has time to prepare for it. There are other godly men in the congregation whose gifts would enable them to perform this office effectively, but they are working at other things during the week and support him in order that he may perform this and other pastoral functions well. The minister has an obligation to prepare thoroughly for the hour of worship.

Orders of worship are developed in each church according to the tradition in which it stands. Whatever the sequence, there should be sound theological reasons for it, and it should be designed for the needs and capacities of the people who unite in the service. This involves familiarity with the history and literature of public worship, the development of a theology of worship, and efforts, along with the church officers, to arrange a good liturgy for the church. It involves a knowledge of the everyday lives of the people who gather for worship so that what is said and done may be relevant. In some of the less conventional churches of our time this is symbolized by having a place in the order of worship for members to present concerns. One may speak of a parents' meeting at the school, another of a housing protest gathering, or clothing drive. Still others may mention persons who are ill or a member overseas on a mission. This may be helpful, but it may be objectionable to some congregations and may not take the place of the awareness developed as the pastor goes in and out among the people, or consults with the members who minister to one another.

Also involved is the careful preparation of *public prayers,* whether they are chosen from the church's treasury or composed by the pastor. One who is to lead a people in speaking to God should plan as carefully as one who is to lead a delegation to the President of the United States. He must also bear in mind that his public prayers will have an important effect on the private devotional lives of church members. Nor can he forget that the prayers of the church should cover the whole range of human need, aspiration, and obligation. Only careful preparation can take these things into consideration and leave the moments of prayer wholly centered upon God.

A printed or mimeographed order has some value for worship. It makes material easily available for congregational participation, and enables the pastor to be selective. It eliminates the need for giving hymn numbers. Where cost is an important factor or there is no one but the pastor to operate a mimeograph, material may be made available in a selection of orders printed and pasted in hymnals, or the pews may be furnished with a service book, such as *The Book of Common Prayer, The Book of Common Worship,* or *A Book of Worship for Free Churches.* Hymns may be posted on number-boards or announced. There is no reason why spoken instructions should be more intrusive than written ones.

Notices of the activities of the fellowship may be equally acceptable or objectionable in written or spoken form as either may bid for the worshipers' attention at the wrong time. Many churches are now publishing the notices on a separate sheet given out after worship or mailed to homes of the congregation. A minister may, however, become too fastidious about announcements, to the detriment of the congregation's family feeling. He needs the insight of one of America's great architects who watched a hundred choristers in three choirs enter in processional. He thought just the right family touch was added by a junior boy who somehow got in line without a gown!

Ushers who know their business are an asset in any service. They move quietly and only when necessary, and learn an expressive language of simple gesture, rather than speech. They know members, their needs and preferences, and are sincerely pleased to greet them. They see in each newcomer a man or woman God loves for whom the church has a message. They are unfailingly courteous, but firm about such things as seating periods. They are alert and know what to do about lighting and ventilation, and can move unobtrusively and effectively when emergencies arise. The precision with which they function when the offering is received testifies silently to their feeling of the importance of participation in worship. They agree to dress in clothing that does not call attention to them, but each wears a simple flower or a " feather carnation," furnished by the church. They have a plan for dealing with fire or panic. They enjoy their tasks, are in their places on assigned Sundays without fail, and are prepared to recruit and train replacements.

4. Music

Music is an important part of worship. It may provide a beautiful expression of our love for God. It offers opportunity for all to participate in hymn singing and for many to use their gifts in choral music. Watching the faces of a congregation singing or caught up in the soaring beauty of a fine anthem, one can believe there is singing in heaven.

There are times, of course, when other reflections intrude! The quality of church music may be incredibly bad. This is not necessary. It may be *well chosen* for its high purpose. There is usually a high school choral leader and a piano teacher or two near the church who will be happy to assist the music committee and volunteer organist in setting standards. Most of the good schools of music will be happy to supply lists of fine music for choirs of modest ability. Dependence on the lists of one music publisher is unwise.

When the church employs an organist and choirmaster, it should make sure he has good taste in music and the wisdom to consult with the pastor about words, at least until he fully understands the viewpoint of the church. Then the official board should back him when he makes his choices, turning a pleasant face, but deaf ear, toward occasional demands for the cheap and sentimental or the merely old. It should be recognized by all that it is a time-consuming process to discover fresh and vital music. A church that can afford a full-time musician will expect him to give many hours to finding the right anthems.

Quality of choral performance depends to a large degree upon the director. The same choir of adults or children will sound completely different under two successive leaders. The effective choral director communicates his feeling of the necessity for offering something fine to God, his confidence that the group can do this, his determination that the offering shall be as nearly perfect as possible, his concern that each member of the choir be regular in attendance at rehearsals and in church. If a director has potential, the music committee may help him develop through sending him to conferences and by offering to underwrite summer training in a music school or choral center. If he lacks essential qualities, they can begin planning for a good replacement when conditions are right.

A competent director will need support from the official board in setting high standards, and insisting, as he will, that those absent from a rehearsal shall not sing the following Sunday.

Personal growth on the part of singers may be expected under good direction. Voices will improve, taste in music will be better; but most important, adults and children will participate in worship and have the joy of offering something worthwhile to God. Occasionally the director will have to find a way to discourage an adult from joining a choir or to persuade an individual with a particularly raucous voice to serve the Lord in some other way. The ego seems to be intimately related to the singing voice, so that this can be a delicate business in which the leader will need support and sometimes help from the music committee. Annual auditions may help. So may the offer of another demanding place of service. It may be wise to avoid general invitations to join the choir. If there is a large choir, the director may work tactfully with the offending person whose "voice must be kept soft to blend with smaller voices."

Choir placement in a back balcony, where this is available, frees the director for more overt leadership, enables the choir to take a natural part in worship and give attention to the preaching, and guards the service against the distractions that may come from a choir at the front. When there is a very large choir under a director who can assure complete involvement in worship and maintain discipline, the inspiration afforded by their visible presence may be worth the disadvantages. This may also be true when there is a divided chancel in which the choir does not face the congregation, though this arrangement which divides the choral group, fine as it was for monks singing to one another and God, leaves something to be desired musically.

Youth choirs are valuable in that they involve young people and children in the leadership of worship, even though their offering may be only a response. If there are age-group choirs, the average boy or girl may spend most Sundays in a service of worship through the most formative years. Under good direction, these groups may be musical organizations bringing something of real worth to the services. In churches where there are several services they may be indispensable. A recent development is the establishment of bell choirs, especially for boys whose voices are changing.

The choirmaster can give better direction if he does not also have to play the organ. Except for the occasional genius, a person performing both tasks will be more gifted at one of them, and even the genius has trouble holding up the tone quality of a large choir and keeping the signals clear if he must give attention to an organ. This is borne out by the fact that brilliant organist-directors almost always secure an organist if they are to conduct a cantata. It is, of course, better to have a good musician perform in both capacities than to have two persons, one of whom has mediocre powers. And it is better to have no musician at all than to have a choirmaster without faith and Christian motivation.

Organs are very expensive instruments and may be costly to maintain. Quality is more important than quantity. The organist and music committee will wish to have a consultation with at least one outstanding organist before an order is placed. While organists usually prefer wind instruments, some of these are definitely inferior to the best electronic organs in the same price range. If there are musicians in the congregation, they will prefer a good piano to an electronic organ in its price range. If the hard choice must be made between employment of a better organist or purchase of a better organ, the increased expenditure for the organist will do more for the services.

5. Times of Worship

Times of worship in Protestant churches can no longer be taken for granted. For a long time one was safe in assuming that morning worship would be at eleven o'clock, with the evening service at seven forty-five or a vesper service at five in the afternoon. The church school began at nine forty-five A.M., just before morning worship, or afterward at noon. In Episcopal and Lutheran churches there would be an early Communion at eight o'clock.

Sunday morning services may now occur at nine and eleven o'clock, or nine thirty and eleven, or even eight, nine, ten, and eleven o'clock. Church schools for children may run concurrently with worship hours. Then youth classes come in afternoon or evening session connected with youth fellowships. Sometimes entire families may be expected to attend church school at one hour and church the previous or succeeding hour.

The time for worship is occasionally set at ten thirty A.M., with children accompanying their parents. They are dismissed at eleven o'clock for church school. In some of these churches, the service is planned to stop at eleven thirty A.M., and adults are expected to attend classes until noon or twelve fifteen. A good many churches provide nursery care during services, and if a church school session is not in progress, offer a program to which primary and junior children may go after twenty minutes' to a half hour's participation in public worship. There is increasing awareness that small children need the experience of public worship with their families and the whole fellowship, but develop wrong attitudes toward worship when required to sit through a sermon they do not understand. The regular participation of youth choirs in services has greatly increased the interest and attendance of young people.

Sunday afternoon or evening services are now the exception rather than the rule except in the South. Where they are held, it is usually assumed that the attendance will be much smaller than in the morning. This is interesting in view of the new afternoon and evening services developing in Roman Catholic churches. More experiments are needed in this area, especially in view of the large number of persons so employed that they can rarely attend in the morning, or may be prevented from doing so a third of the time by swing-shift jobs. A good many churches do have programs for young people and young adults which include vital services of worship planned by the participants. The Sunday evening hours are also used for small-group activities involving young married couples without children, and others of all ages without parental responsibility.

Weekday services once occurred rather generally on Wednesday evenings. These usually represented a development — and in the later stages often a rather sterile one — of the Wesleyan prayer meetings. They were originally intended as an opportunity for group Bible study and prayer and a vital exchange of experience by growing Christians. They became formal services, duplicating those on Sundays, or degenerated into little "in" groups, repeating pious clichés. However, the original idea was a good one and in many churches today, on Wednesday evenings or other evenings, some afternoons, and even at six or seven in the mornings, there are weekly gatherings limited to ten or twelve persons, leagued together for

Bible study, prayer, the sharing of Christian experience, and the discussion of problems faced in daily life.

Weekday services of worship are often designed for particular groups. Noonday services are useful in downtown areas and near industrial plants. Early services before school attract a surprising number of teen-agers, particularly during Lent or Advent. Services are held in plants or large business houses, in hospitals and homes, prisons and detention centers, shopping plazas and airports, drive-in movies, picnic grounds, and campsites. Healing services are conducted regularly in many places, with the people in attendance reporting both spiritual and physical blessings. Services of general interest may be scheduled for a regular evening each week. Downtown, this may be on a shopping night; in the suburbs, before or after some other meetings.

Open churches or chapels are more and more found to be available for personal devotional use during the week. There is a sound tradition that Protestants worship together in church on Sunday and in families and alone at home during the week. God is not to be found in church more easily than at home. But one must face the fact that this depends on the home! In these days of glass walls and room dividers, there are not many places that offer real privacy. A quiet church pew may be a very attractive place for devotion. Conversely, a great many people live alone, and get something of a family feeling as they bow in a church where one or two others are praying silently, or where many others have gathered for prayer.

6. Funerals

The funeral or memorial service is a service of worship. Christian families are encouraged to use the church when it is convenient. It is usually advisable to have the body present in a simple casket which should be closed for the service. The presence of the body frankly recognizes its importance in human life and helps relatives to face the earthly finality of death. The closing of the casket places attention on God. Funerals have high priority for a pastor, but he may expect morticians to set no dates or hours without consulting him first. He will find them cooperative if he indicates the hours of the day when he prefers to take funerals.

The service should affirm the Word of God's love and power

in Christ. This is done effectively by the reading of Scripture, a brief exposition of the gospel, and prayers. The prayers include praise of God and thanksgiving for his gift of Christ and the Christian hope. There is further thanksgiving for the gift of life to the one who is gone, together with the blessings he enjoyed in infancy, youth, and maturity, the grace that touched his life, the persons who have enriched his days, the blessings he brought to others, and the new life upon which he has entered. A sense of victory will pervade this part of the prayer. Then there are prayers for all present, that they may enter fully into life, and for the bereaved, that they may be comforted. The conclusion comes with rejoicing in the communion of the saints, and the benediction. There should be a note of victory in the air as people leave a Christian funeral service.

The pastor will find that the ancient prayers of the church are of help. He may turn to *The Book of Common Prayer, The Book of Common Worship,* the *Common Service Book of the Lutheran Church, A Book of Worship for Free Churches,* or *Christian Worship: A Service Book.* Most poetry does not stand up well against the words of Scripture and age-old words of prayer. Unfortunate suggestions from sentimental people will be avoided if the pastor never uses poetry at funerals. At the grave he will be well advised to confine himself to the brief words of the interment service.

7. Weddings

When young people decide to be married they will come to see the pastor. If the youth program of the church is properly designed, they will know that they ought, if possible, to come some months before the date chosen for the wedding. When outsiders unknown to the minister appear, he will make no commitment until there has been adequate time for conference. If the way is clear, arrangements for the wedding may be facilitated by the use of a marriage record card. The minister fills out this card during the first interview. It will include the name, address, and phone number of the bride and of the groom, as well as specifications regarding the organist, soloist (if any), the number of bridesmaids, ushers, and other participants, the names of the official witnesses, and plans for the reception if the church is involved. There will also be a place where the license number, date, and place of issue may be entered when the minister receives this document. He should make his entry before performing the service, as many states have waiting periods, and the act of writing the date of issue may prevent a serious mistake. If he lives in a state that requires that the entire license be mailed back to the issuing office, as in the case of New York, he may protect himself against the charge of failing to file by sending with the license a self-addressed postcard acknowledging receipt of the document, with a place for the county clerk's signature. This postcard, when returned, may be filed with the marriage record card.

Wedding suggestions may be mimeographed. There will be diagrams of the wedding party at the front of the church, entering in procession, and leaving. There will be instructions for ushers concerning seating of guests and family, checking on the presence of all members of the wedding party, the handling (where necessary) of the white canvas aisle cover, and the signal to be given the organist when all is in readiness. The use of appropriate music will be discussed, with explanation of the necessity of using the church organist, his part in recommending music and his fees. It will be noted that photographers are not to be conspicuous in the church at any time, and must not intrude upon the service. Costs will be discussed, with a warning against extravagance. Members should not be charged for use of the church or chapel, and some congregations offer facilities freely to all. The sexton's fee may be related to the number invited as this affects the amount of his work.

The rehearsal may be expedited by beginning with all the members of the wedding party taking their places at the front. This is followed by a rehearsal of the service, then of the exit march, and finally of the entrance march. At this point the group sits down and asks any questions. The pastor's goal is a service of worship in which the couple is free of concern for details, and able to think about their dedication to each other before God. For this reason he will not encourage the memorization of vows or anything else that may direct attention to the mechanics of the service.

The minister will wish to give the couple a *certificate of marriage*. He may use in the service a white booklet that contains the certificate and the entire marriage service, or he may prefer a suitably engraved certificate in a folder. Both are available through denominational bookstores at modest cost.

Chapter IX

Nurture

The church will devote a major portion of its time to nurture if it is true to its Lord's teaching and example. Our Lord is still saying, "Feed my sheep." Those who enter upon the life in Christ are beginning a long pilgrimage in which they need the guidance and support of other members of the family. The church in our time is being reminded of an often neglected heritage by the amazing results of a gathered family environment in ending drug addiction under the auspices of the Synanon movement. There is much that we can do for one another as the Spirit of Christ leads us toward maturity.

1. Visitations for Pastoral Care

a. *Members may visit* other members as a part of the program of mutual nurture in a church. Geographical districts may be established, with the membership commission or a board taking responsibility for arrangements. A map is mounted on wallboard and a pin is placed at the location of each family in the church. Then, district boundaries are drawn, establishing areas with fifteen to thirty homes. Each district is given a number. The church district number is thenceforth included in the record of each family. As people move over the years, districts may be divided into two, or two districts may be merged.

Responsibility for calling on members should be accepted by the official board members or assigned to another board or the membership commission. Provision should be made for at least one yearly visit to each home in addition to any financial canvass. The person who makes this pastoral call should never be assigned the same home for a financial call. Sometimes a board or commission will make evening calls and enlist a women's committee to visit in the afternoons to reach older people and shut-ins. The easiest plan to administer is also the most effective. It involves the assignment of one commission or board member to take pastoral responsibility for each district. He calls at the homes and makes written reports each month to an officer of the board or commission. This officer gives the pastor information gleaned from reports, and at the pastor's request before a monthly meeting, asks visitors to call on particular families during the next month. The pastor may be directly notified by the visitor of any urgent need, and will in turn directly inform the visitor of the hospitalization or death of anyone in the visitor's district.

The pastor will regard it as one of his high privileges to train the groups that make calls. In time there will be other members of the church who can do this as well, or better, than he. Part of the training will be regular meetings for discussion of the task and reports on calls made. A wonderful booklet of sixty-three pages which may be placed in the hands of each caller, is *How to Make Pastoral Calls,* by Russell L. Dicks (The Bethany Press, 1962).

There is one church (which has quarterly Communion services) in which each official board member calls on the members in his district before Communions. Members have permanent Communion tokens which are handed in at the service each quarter, stamped with the date of attendance, and returned to the members before the next Communion by the person who calls. When a token is not used, the official board member goes again after the service to collect it. Needless to say, the percentage of members in attendance at this large church is much above average. Many churches do not go this far, but do have an organized visitation by officers or volunteers before Worldwide Communion in the fall, often including a distribution of tokens to be signed and presented at the service. Others mail tokens before this, and sometimes before each Communion, frequently supplementing the mailings with telephone calls from the district visitors or others.

b. *The pastor's visitations* are for the purpose of continuing the conversation about the Word of God's love, carried on in the pulpit last Sunday and to go on in the pulpit next Sunday. Some things may be said and done in the pulpit which are inappropriate in the home, and the reverse is true, but the whole conversation must be consistent or none of it will be effective. Since the pastor does all the talking in the pulpit, he will do most of the listening in the home, but he will ask the right questions, and he will listen expertly and with the inner ear. Upon installation in a church a pastor should plan to call in every home of the parish as soon as possible. This may take two months or two years, but he will plan the number of calls necessary each week until this essential task is done. He will begin with a list of shut-ins, then call on officers' families, then move routinely through the neighborhoods. Once the first visitation has been made, plans for other calls will depend upon the size and attitude of the congregation, the number of special calls and counseling interviews found to be necessary, the number of regular contacts in the activities of the church, and the pastor's total responsibility. In any event, a system of visitation should be continuous, lest dialogue become monologue!

The time for home visitation will be the second half of the afternoon and the early evening. The exact hours convenient in any parish will differ according to the employment of the people. One must learn their patterns of working, eating and sleeping, shopping and recreation. In industrial communities, the workers are usually at home by four thirty or five o'clock, and about half of them, being on shift work, will be at home afternoons about a third of the time. The business or professional man is often available only in the evening or on Saturday or Sunday afternoon. Afternoon calls may usually be made in less time, and by observation one may learn where he will be welcome right up to six o'clock. In evening visitation it is important to go on only as long as one is alert. Much time is wasted after the minister gets too tired.

Many pastors do all visitation by appointment. This usually assures the presence of the entire family, sets the time limits of the call, and makes it possible to use more of an evening, as the last call may begin later. It avoids intrusion upon a party or a room-painting project. People also tend to view the visit in a more serious light, and often have topics they wish to discuss. Over against this, calling without appointment has several advantages. It enables the pastor to adjust the length of the call to the circumstances, staying ten minutes in one place, an hour in another. It results in more spontaneity, and if occasionally the pastor finds all the furniture in the middle of the floor, the unconventional scene may become a cherished mutual memory to be laughed over for years. It relieves the minister of the considerable pressure that builds up in appointment calling when people delay the parting guest, or the unforeseen fouls up the schedule. Ministers working with business and professional men often arrange to visit them briefly in their offices or have lunch with them. Several are riding commuter trains one or two days a week in order to talk with men who leave home early and return late, and are busy all day.

House calls are important when the pastor learns or senses that a problem has arisen. In most communities an illness serious enough to suggest a call usually results in hospitalization, but there are other things. The pastor may go when there is continual absence from church services, a conflict with other members, evidence of personality disorder or family disintegration, the loss of a job, or other emergency. Often he cannot bring the matter up, but he can make himself available. Usually, people are more than willing to talk about their difficulties.

When some real or imagined injury has been received from the church or one of its members or groups, the pastor may have to accept an unfair attack or a torrent of abuse. He needs to remember that if he holds to his pastoral mission with sincere concern for the member and does not become defensive, all but those who are emotionally disturbed to a serious degree will eventually come around to a more constructive frame of mind.

c. *Visits to the hospital* will come at the head of the pastor's calling list.

The pastor arriving in a new parish will wish to become familiar at once with the hospitals serving his people. He will learn where he may leave his coat and hat, and when he is most welcome. He may find a register of patients arranged by religious affiliation, or he may work through the council of churches to get one established. Often arrangements can be made to have volunteers at the hospital notify each pastor when a member of his church is admitted. When these aids are not available and the patient does not tell the pastor, the word usually comes through a friend. The minister who receives this word with obvious appreciation, even if he has already heard of the hospitalization, will be eagerly helped in the future. The man who pretends omniscience a few times will be left without an important source of information.

Some churches mail each member, annually, a postage-paid reply card on which imminent hospitalization or other needs may be checked and sent to the church office. The card also carries a telephone number and a printed notice suggesting that it be kept in a convenient place. Bulletin notices remind members that the pastor may be reached by telephone. Despite all efforts, one occasionally meets the contradictory behavior of the sick person who hides the fact of his illness or hospitalization, yet is greatly pleased when called upon, or full of complaint when there are no calls. The pastor will recognize a hunger for love and a deep-seated sense of worthlessness in such persons, which offer an unusual opportunity for a Christian ministry.

Once he has established the fact of hospitalization, the pastor must determine a course of action. This is simpler if he has an overall policy related to the size of his responsibilities and the location of hospitals. Most men call in hospitals at least two afternoons a week, on a regular schedule. They will, of course, go as soon as possible upon first hearing of a serious illness or sudden emergency. They may call more frequently when a person or his family is in special need, but they will also be aware of the danger of spiritually pauperizing Christians by making them dependent upon a man rather than upon God.

Today not many persons stay in a hospital more than a few days. The pastor may be of most help the afternoon or evening before an operation while a person's mind is clear and faith, or its absence, is felt. If the pastor has done his work effectively while the person was well, a brief visit will be adequate. He will let his friend take the lead in any conversation, then gather up their mutual faith in a prayer. If the caller and patient are largely strangers, the task is difficult but still possible. On the day of surgery the patient is half asleep and the pastor's chief usefulness may be as a support to relatives. Some pastors successfully prepare church friends of the family for this service and arrange for them to spend the period of the operation with the relatives. After surgery and on medical floors when a patient is very ill, the pastor slips quietly into the room for a brief prayer, and is gone. Hospital prayers, like everything else the pastor does, are full of the Word of God's love and power in Christ. He will say what he believes the person will want to say to God in this light, avoiding particulars that may be disturbing.

When convalescence is slow or the condition chronic, the patient often desires frequent and extended calls. The pastor meets this need by dropping in each time he is in the hospital. If his friend does not follow an exchange of greetings with some comments, he will be prepared with a story of a recent event that will at once introduce something new for the patient to think about and offer him an acceptable framework for expressing some of his feelings or questions. Because he knows that his pastor, like his doctor, is about serious business and cannot stay very long, he is more likely to come out quickly with what he wants to say. The results of their conversation and its implications may be gathered up in their prayer. After several visits, the pastor will know which of the church members may fruitfully undertake a ministry of longer visits on a regular schedule, and he will make arrangements. He will do this also in connection with shut-ins at home and in convalescent homes.

2. Pastoral Counseling

a. *Counseling* has always been a part of the pastoral function. Many of the needs that will be brought to the minister's attention may now be met more effectively by others. It is his duty to know who the others are, how their help may be enlisted, and how the person who consults him may be led to the proper source of help. The minister will wish to know as much as he can about psychology and counseling techniques. The more he knows, the better he will understand himself and the less he will be inclined to be an amateur psychiatrist. His unique function is to communicate the revelation of God's love and power set forth in Christ. Often this is just what troubled persons and families need, but the proclamation can rarely take the form of an announcement. It reaches them first in the pastor's personal interest, his acceptance of them as they are, his willingness to listen and ask helpful questions, his obvious assurance through everything that God loves them and will help them.

In his first parish the average minister will have a rather limited number of people confide in him, and this will usually occur following a conversation about some "church business" or during a visit at a home or in the hospital. If a man is ready for helpful counseling, it shows in his sermons. If he deals well with those who come, others will follow but this may take several years, and forcing will not help. Some men never get beyond this point without special training, and some with much training are too anxious – and people know it. It may be that a man's ministry is complete with very little of this counseling. He may be greatly reducing the need for this remedial action by his pastoral leadership and personal and group relationships. When a famous pastoral counselor recently retired, he revealed that over twenty-five years he had seen only an average of ten persons a week. Many pastors will eventually find themselves budgeting five or six hours a week for counseling, and a few may have to allow more. This time must be taken from that budgeted for visitation and the minister will have to decide, with prayer and hard thought, how to keep a balance. It is flattering when people seek one out, the needs are obvious, the results often wonderful. Cure is usually more spectacular than prevention, but not necessarily more important.

The thoughtful counselor will find reasonable ways of saving time. The intervals between interviews may be lengthened, referrals may be arranged earlier without giving a sense of rejection, disturbed people calling in the middle of the night may get more help if they accept an appointment for two o'clock the next afternoon. Despite every effort, however, the pastoral counselor must devote time each week to this service. More people in distress turn to him than to doctors or psychiatrists or social workers, and he must do what he can – often undertaking things beyond his knowledge and skill because no one else is available. In this situation it is well for him to remember that the love and power that entered the world in Jesus

Christ can do some remarkable things, despite the pastor's limitations.

b. *When someone dies,* the pastor will wish to visit the family at once. If the word has not come from the family, it may be wise to telephone first and ask when it may be convenient for the relatives to see him. In making calls at the time of death, the pastor allows the bereaved persons to take the lead in conversation. The first call helps to express the solidarity of the Christian fellowship even though nothing may be said beyond a word of heartfelt sympathy and a closing prayer. No effort is made to reason against expressions of doubt and rebellion. The prayer includes thanksgiving for the life of the one who is gone, for the love and power of God which turned the death of Christ from a dark and terrible event into a blessing for us all, and for the promise of Jesus that he has gone to prepare a place for us and that we shall be with him always. The second call, at the formal visiting hours, will be brief and designed primarily to express again personal concern and the sympathy of the church. The call or calls after the funeral may offer more help. If possible, the grieving person is encouraged to talk about the one who is gone and the things they did together. After a time the conversation may come around to doubts and feelings of guilt or rebellion and plans for the future. This may have to wait for subsequent visits.

The pastor may choose, as soon as possible, a member of the congregation most likely to be able to help. This person will be asked to call regularly for a time, getting in touch with the minister if serious problems arise. The visitor may arrange to bring the bereaved to church and gently lead toward participation in a small church group. At some point the recovering sorrower may be asked to undertake a personal ministry to someone else. Thus the mutual ministry of the congregation grows.

c. *When people ask the pastor to officiate at their wedding* he will wish to talk with them. The minister may wish to use a questionnaire designed for initial interviews. At the least, he will wish to bring up the physical, social, economic, and religious aspects of the life they plan together. In connection with the physical, he may lend them a good book, inquire whether they plan to discuss this subject with their physician, and offer them a card of introduction to the local planned parenthood center. If there are questions, he will not avoid them, but he need not undertake a major contribution in this area. In connection with the personal and social, he may help them explore their temperaments and inclinations, as well as their relationships to their parents and other relatives and friends, as these may affect their mutual relations. He will have them examine their likenesses and differences, their preferences in the use of leisure time, their ways of handling frustrations, their goals and dreams, and their attitude toward children. He will bring up the subject of budget and their plans for financing their joint venture, making certain that each becomes aware of the other's attitudes in such matters. The importance of mutual faith will become apparent to them in the course of the conversation. There will be some discussion of their convictions and, if necessary, exploration of differences. Plans for church relationship, for membership in a small group of Christian couples, and for prayer together will be given attention.

If, in any of this, there are signs of difficulty, the pastor may wish to arrange further interviews with the couple or see each of them separately or lead them to accept referral to persons who can help them. Occasionally, on the basis of discoveries in the first interview, a couple may decide to postpone marriage or to give up the idea. The minister will not, of course, tell them what to do. There may be situations in which he will feel he cannot preside at the wedding. If the reasons are based on the rules of his communion, he can usually determine this by a few questions at the outset. If they are based on his judgment about the wisdom of the marriage, he should give his answer as soon as possible, making it clear why he takes his position and what alternatives are before them.

3. Devotional Life

a. *Efforts to encourage personal and family devotions* may include preparation of special material and promotion of available resources. The pastor may prepare an annual booklet of Scripture readings for each day, related to his sermons. Sometimes these readings are published weekly in a church paper. A group may gather material and mimeograph a suggested guide for family devotions. People who cannot be persuaded to use anything else will use material prepared by friends. The church library may be stocked with devotional classics, ancient and modern. They are more likely to be read if the pastor refers to them in sermons, or mention is made of them in a weekly publication. This is also true of devotional guides such as *Today* and *The Upper Room,* which may be distributed from display stands in vestibules and halls with a coin box nearby for contributions toward their cost. If the cost is noted, the contributions will usually cover it. Families may also be directed to devotional material in church school quarterlies. Promotional efforts by pastoral visitors who are themselves using material will have real effect.

b. *Small groups* have been mentioned in the chapter on worship. They may become the most important elements in a church program. Limited to about twelve persons, they may be called research groups, koinonia groups, Bible study groups, and prayer groups. They are started when the pastor finds three or four persons or several couples interested. The attempt to start a whole system of small groups by putting every member in one is doomed to failure at the outset. If the first group proves vital, it will grow and there will be requests for others. One effective way to give people a taste of small-group experience is to invite up to twelve persons for an all-day retreat at the church. Sometimes those invited may be the members of a board or committee or a social group. If the program is well planned, some will wish to try a regular small group.

Leadership is provided at first by the pastor. Later, there may be a chairman chosen from the group, or the group may disband, with each one or several members becoming the center of a new group. Ministerial leadership should not be required after a good start, though the pastor will always wish to be involved in one group and will occasionally visit others, holding himself in readiness to attend when asked.

The program usually extends for one and a half to two hours. The group may decide to change the format from time to time. It may begin with silent prayer. Then there may be a period of Bible study in which a passage is read and discussed in terms of its meaning and application, with members bringing up problems from their own lives and speaking of ways Christ has helped them. Occasionally, the group may prefer to use a book on Christian thought and life as the basis for discussion, reading a chapter in advance and working through it together. Sometimes, after thorough grounding, they may wish to read a novel or play at home and discuss Christian answers to problems it raises. If these approaches are used, the members should be committed to enough independent Bible study so that there is adequate Biblical reference in the meetings. Group Bible study, enriched by the outside reading and experience of the members, is the most helpful basis of continual gatherings. The meetings usually close with a period of prayers in which each one eventually learns to take part.

Sometimes, as a result of their discussions, the persons in the group decide to covenant with God and one another to do certain things. They may agree to spend fifteen minutes a day in personal devotions. Possibly all will read the same passages of Scripture. Tithing of income may be another discipline. There may be discussion and agreement about how each may best help with nurture in the church and witness in the world. This may lead to further commitment. One of these groups spent a whole year preparing a prayer notebook, which was then mimeographed for wide distribution. Another developed for publication a volume of choice selections from a devotional classic. A third provided dedicated leadership for two ventures of the congregation: a storefront mission and a migrant ministry, as well as workers for a better-housing effort in the community.

Real fellowship develops as a group continues. The members come to care about one another and become a real family in Christ. Though there are, as yet, few churches in which most of the members are in these vital groups, their influence upon the life of the churches is out of all proportion to the number involved, and their promise is great.

c. *Retreats* are closely related to the small-group movement, and may be said to have shaped it. Protestant interest in retreats has been stimulated by the Iona Movement in Scotland, Kirkridge in America, and like centers in Germany, Italy, France, India, and New Zealand. The essence of a retreat is a time and place in which attention is directed to God. Part of the experience is solitary, part in company with other Christians. A weekend or two-day period is better than one day because of the cumulative effect, but one day can be very profitable. Economic reasons and family considerations make the one-day experience more attractive to persons attending for the first time. There is also the advantage of complete simplicity of arrangements. Each may bring food ready to eat at one or two meals. The hours may be from seven A.M to three P.M. for men, or from ten A.M. to five P.M. for women or couples. No one is accepted for less than the whole period.

The place chosen should be protected from intrusion by location or arrangement. There should be places where each of the twelve people and the leader may have complete privacy during solitary periods. Natural beauty is an asset, but not a necessity. There should be a place suitable for group worship, which may be reserved for this alone, and another place for meetings. A place too familiar may cause intrusive associations. A retreat or conference center is ideal. Another church may provide a good setting. The home church may do very well if someone else volunteers to protect the group against intrusion.

A typical program for a one-day retreat may include an opening period of worship followed by the leader's outline of the purpose and plan. There may be three divisions of the day, each including a presentation by the leader, a group discussion of the topic, and a period of silence when each goes off alone to read the Bible, meditate, and pray. The period of silence should be the longest period in each cycle. With new groups the silent time should be fairly short in the first cycle, and somewhat longer in each successive cycle. One of the leader's tasks is to prepare retreatants to use these quiet periods, which are frightening to many people. Some will need very explicit instructions about what to do. Meals may be opportunities for informal fellowship. In longer retreats, silence may be observed or someone may read to the group at meals. A service of worship may conclude the day.

A serious danger of retreats inadequately led is the morbid increase of introspection. It is essential that attention be directed primarily to God, and not to the self, and that sinfulness be faced always in the light of grace. God knows what he is doing when, with the cross, he confronts us at once with our sinfulness and his grace. It is also important that no impression be created that God is to be found primarily in a "holy" place rather than in the workaday world. Jesus was as aware of the Father in the house of Simon the Pharisee as at Caesarea Philippi.

Our Lord did take time for retreats in the days of his flesh.

We do well to follow him in this, as in other things. We also need to remember that he has provided us with one day in seven when the atmosphere of retreat may pervade our homes and our lives. The church will wish to encourage wise use of *the Lord's Day* — as he used it — for worship and good fellowship and deeds of kindness.

4. Fellowship

Fellowship must be more than a word in the church. Christian people should come together and develop a sense of belonging together. This happens in worship and in efforts for mutual growth and witness, but often the worship and common activity occur only after some experience of Christian fellowship. They are always richer when the people engaged in them know one another in social relationships. Jesus went to parties and often had meals with friends. The social hall and dining table are early fixtures in the church and have a legitimate place.

a. *Some inclusive occasions* are necessary. The whole congregation should be invited to sit down to dinner two or three times a year. Some nonsense is a good thing, but the program will have content related to the purposes of the church. When business must be transacted, it will be carefully prepared and presented so that tedious efforts to supply information or clarify purposes will not be necessary.

Most fellowship must occur in smaller groups; indeed, really personal relations can only develop in this way. It is not important that each member of a congregation know every other member. It is essential that each know some members well. Since people are not all alike, we cannot expect them to relate to one another at the level sought in the small personal groups we have discussed. Jesus had only one group of twelve out of at least five hundred interested persons. Others were devoted to him, but were not ready for the more intense experience.

b. *Older members* should have at least one group, such as a senior fellowship, to which they may belong when other activity is not possible. Those well enough may be provided with transportation to the monthly meetings and may have a number to call if they wish a ride to church. The monthly meetings may begin with a program related to the Christian life, followed by refreshments in a party atmosphere. A fifteen- or twenty-minute service of worship in the church or chapel, with a brief sermon by the pastor, will be especially appreciated by those who cannot regularly attend worship. Some of these groups have a monthly paper mimeographed and mailed to members so that the shut-ins may keep in touch with the others. The paper carries news of the church, information about members of the senior fellowship, reviews of new books in the church library, brief articles by members, and requests for prayer which may come from church members, action groups, and missionaries. Some groups also circulate Home Department magazines and copies of *Today* or *The Upper Room* and offer to supply books from the church or public libraries.

Through the Blind Association or the Library of Congress, arrangements are made for members with limited vision to have, at no expense, a talking book. This is a special record player. A regular supply of Bible readings and of the latest books of all sorts is available on records from the Library of Congress without cost. Members who cannot afford a radio or television set may be furnished with one that remains church property and is serviced on call. Some groups relate infirm members living alone to services of the visiting nurse association, including the "Meals on Wheels" program, or, themselves, supply warm evening meals where necessary. Shut-ins are visited monthly by a person who becomes a friend, sends small Christmas gifts and an Easter card, and occasionally takes a little surprise. The services for the senior fellowship are usually provided by a group of women, with resources furnished by the church, including extra liability insurance on cars used.

c. *Programs for women and for men* are discussed in section b on "organizations" in Chapter IV. Help in planning local fellowship and service and in introducing women or men to wider Christian fellowship may be secured from denominational and ecumenical agencies. There may be district and national meetings and training schools, and excellent printed materials.

d. *Couples groups* are comparatively recent additions to church programs, but they, too, may now receive help from national groups in most communions. They are the products in one sense of the feeling that in our busy, impersonal, and insecure world, family life is very precious. Husbands and wives wish to be together and to share more experiences. They may have no interest in going out alone to a men's or women's meeting, but they will go together to a couples group.

A group may come into being when the pastor or a couple familiar with the pattern invites up to twelve couples for a buffet supper or for dessert. The eating is leisurely, and is followed by a relaxed period in which everyone becomes acquainted. This may involve asking each to follow the pastor or hosts in giving a personal biography, including how they met husband or wife, and something of their church experience. Usually, a good deal of interest and fun can be expected from this, and it may be guided into a good informal discussion of religion and family life or something equally pertinent. The evening may continue with a game or two: something like "Twenty Questions" is useful. For young married people each evening out may be a charge against a limited budget. The young mother, especially, wants some fun and a chance to forget responsibility for a little while. At the end of the evening it is suggested that the group may wish to meet again the following month; a host and hostess are recruited, and a couple to plan the program. A modest cost for meals is agreed upon, or the hosts are asked to telephone assignments for dishes to be brought by each. Sometimes group baby-sitting is arranged or exchanges are proposed with another couples group.

At the second meeting, the program has the same elements, but a different subject is introduced by a speaker, with discussion following. This time a couple is chosen as chairmen for a year. They will prepare a schedule of hosts and program chairmen for each month. There is no other organization and there are no dues, offerings, or fund-raising activities permitted. The meetings will usually be held in homes. This may limit the size, but there should be a minimum of eight couples, even if people have to sit on the floor. Chairs and card tables should be available at the church, as well as inexpensive table settings for twenty-four in a box or basket, which may be checked in and out and will avoid controversy about silver lost from church supplies. Couples living in small apartments may wish to use church parlors or take responsibility for entertaining during summer months when meetings may be held at outdoor locations.

The attendance of group members at worship, and their participation in Christian service will soon be found to be much above average. Where the groups do not become particularly serious some of their members will be among the recruits for small personal groups and retreats. Further, these people will come to care about one another, lend mutual help in emergencies, and encourage one another to grow in faith. There is another type of couples group which attempts to include all the couples in a church. If it has many more than a dozen couples — and these groups often become monstrous — it will develop, not fellowship, but acquaintance except for the ingroup which will be found to have a maximum of about twelve couples!

e. *Young adults* who are single may have a group that meets each week on Sunday evening and on one other evening. The program is likely to lean heavily to action projects, but should include elements of worship, Christian education, and recreation. A good group is invariably a "marriage bureau" and ought to be. The problem is always a scarcity of men. This is complicated by the tendency of the ablest recruits to pair off — and soon to join the couples! Most effective young adult groups have either, or both, an attractive couple as sponsors and a young minister or student for the ministry as adviser. The exceptions are found where an older pastor has a special gift with this age group, or a spirited young adult emerges to give outstanding leadership.

f. *Young people* may have weekly meetings on Sunday afternoons or evenings. They prefer to have separate fellowships for college-age, high school, and junior high school people. The programs usually include periods for worship, consideration of Christian thought and life, action projects, and recreation, and may last from one to six hours, sometimes including a modest supper. Youth choir rehearsals may be included in this pattern if the church is downtown, or may come at some other time in the week. Social events will involve the groups at varying frequency on weeknights and Saturdays. There may be an annual bus trip to a mission area or to visit a large city and its churches. There is likely to be at least one weekend retreat, and possibly other outings, conferences, and camping trips. Some churches sponsor athletic teams, and scout troops.

g. *Students away from home* may receive regular mailings of church publications and an occasional letter from the pastor or a church officer. They will be invited to a Christmas luncheon at the manse or church and have special invitations for youth meetings that occur when they are at home in the summer. The church may develop a scholarship program, at least for emergency use, and may help in securing summer employment.

h. *Servicemen* should know they are not forgotten. Regular mailings and occasional letters with news of others may help. Christmas gifts may be sent. Special arrangements may be made at the appropriate times for saying "Farewell" and "Welcome home." Notices may be sent to their chaplains.

i. *Travelers* should be encouraged to represent the church when they go away; to carry greetings to other churches and missions and bring back reports and pictures. Most communions will offer help on overseas itineraries if members wish to visit centers of the church's work in other lands.

j. *Out-of-town members* may be classified in two groups: those away temporarily and those who have established permanent residence elsewhere. All will receive regular mailings of church publications. The permanent group will also receive suggestions about churches near them. A pastor in the area may be asked to call on them in the interests of transfer.

5. Christian Education

Christian education is carried forward in almost all activities of a church. It is an important result of the preaching and other pastoral activities, but there must be some specific efforts.

a. *Schools* are found in most churches. A *Sunday church school* will have classes for people of all ages, usually arranged by departments. A curriculum for the Sunday church school is suggested by denominational leaders, though each church is expected to make adaptations. The course is usually planned as a whole to cover the full compass of Christian faith and life as it may be apprehended at different age levels. There are good books for pupils and books or magazines for parents. Educators are deeply impressed with the part the home must play in Christian education and have been trying to develop materials helpful to parents. These emphasize that the church school can only help the home and cannot be the primary place of education in the faith.

Some churches have been experimenting with courses for various age groups. Several have worked out demanding programs for high school students, offering solid work in Bible, theology, church history, and other world views and religions, with consideration of sex and Christian marriage, vocation and Christian stewardship, social and economic justice, and the world mission of the church. Others have produced spectacular results in learning with the use of "teaching machines" in junior and junior high grades. Occasionally one hears of a church that has abolished the Sunday church school altogether, except for adult classes, in the hope of awakening parents to their Christian responsibility as teachers in the home. One who has some knowledge of hundreds of homes will be skeptical of any wisdom in this plan. But it is good to know that able people are putting their minds to work on the problem of Christian education, and to think that any church may develop something of use to all churches.

A special feature of many Sunday church schools is a cradle roll and crib room. Infants are enrolled at birth by a women's committee that calls on new parents, leaving a cradle roll certificate and a book for parents. They arrange for Baptism or dedication and the parents' classes involved. They meet the parents on the day of the service, introducing them to the officer who will lead them to the front of the church. They present them, afterward, with a certificate, and see that the child's name is placed on the proper roll of the church. They invite the parents to use the crib room during church and church school. Another group is responsible for staffing the crib room and keeping it clean and well ventilated and supplied with fresh linens.

Some Sunday church schools are giving special attention to retarded children whose parents and friends prefer to call them exceptional. Classes for boys and girls of limited capacities are now established in a number of places. Often a community of churches will arrange for different congregations to maintain facilities for those with particular problems, or for certain age levels. Talented people with public school experience readily volunteer to train leadership for this rewarding work.

Weekday church schools are maintained by some churches or groups of churches, often using time released by public schools. Classes are planned to supplement the learning in home and Sunday church school, and to supply a minimum knowledge for children not receiving any other Christian education. Most of the programs are under council of churches auspices.

Vacation church schools are extensively maintained. They offer children two to four weeks of classes from nine to twelve in the morning. The denominational curricula are designed to supplement material used on Sundays throughout the year. The longer hours permit intensive work and afford time for interesting projects.

Nursery schools are held on weekday mornings in many churches. Often leadership is on a cooperative basis, with several mothers taking responsibility for specified days. Christian attitudes may reinforce those of the home. Church facilities are often excellent for the purpose, and the mothers, with proper help, may learn much about being Christian parents.

b. *Bible classes* may be established in addition to those in the Sunday church school and the small personal groups. They may include five or five hundred. Weekly or monthly meetings may be held in the early morning before work, at noon, in the late afternoon, or evening. Hundreds of men have been reached by weekly *noonday Bible classes* meeting in connection with lunch or just after it. The Bible talk may follow the singing of several hymns, and lasts fifteen to twenty minutes. Dismissal comes, without fail, at one fifty. The talk is designed to convey solid information, and the speaker is never unaware of the workaday world in which these men are living. He speaks directly to them without notes. The talks may be mimeographed and distributed the following week. Noonday classes for women also meet with a ready response, as do mixed classes, though neither of these usually reaches as many as the men's classes. A number of people will come to these classes who will not, at first, come to church services. The counseling that results from perceptive Bible teaching is a real service, opens evangelistic opportunities, and in turn, keeps the teacher aware of the realities amid which people live.

c. *Study programs* will reach many people. Church nights,

institutes, universities of life, lecture series, and Lenten schools may offer one evening, or successive evenings in one week, or one evening a week for four to eight weeks. One course may be offered, or there may be wide choice. The subjects may be chosen from the whole spectrum of Christian interest. Bible studies are usually most popular, with treatment of prayer a close second. Response is strong for a well-phrased theological or ethical topic. Competent outside speakers add interest, and some churches budget substantial amounts for honoraria. Suppers may be an asset or a liability. Location, age groups, income and habits of families, will affect this. Experiment is the only way to find out. Asking people what they will do by questionnaire or direct inquiry elicits answers that have little relation to what happens.

Study programs may be undertaken by groups, such as a men's club or a circle of women. They agree to read at home and meet from time to time to discuss a subject. Books and study outlines are prepared each year under denominational and ecumenical auspices for themes in the areas of Bible, theology, and the Christian mission at home and abroad. Other books or themes may be chosen, and a study outline prepared by a church committee. The twelve small volumes in the Layman's Theological Library have been used extensively in this way. Books by C. S. Lewis, Elton Trueblood, Reuel Howe, Dietrich Bonhoeffer, and many others, also have been used.

d. *Leadership education* is a necessity in any congregation. Plans may include formal courses and on-the-job training. The courses for teachers and leaders may be given at the church during the church school hour or on a weekday evening. They may continue from fall through spring or be limited to about ten weeks. Printed material may be secured from the denomination, and will cover Bible, theology, the history and mission of the church, the dynamics of human behavior, and tested teaching methods.

The church may decide to arrange most of its formal leadership education in concert with other churches in " schools " or " institutes " that usually function one evening a week for ten weeks in the fall, or at two-week summer institutes held in conference centers. Costs for participants may be borne by the church. Arrangements may be worked out under denominational area guidance or under council of churches sponsorship. These schools may secure expert leadership, as they have access to a large pool of able persons.

Church leaders and teachers will be expected to join regularly in public worship and take advantage of courses and study programs generally available to adults. When there is only one Sunday service with some church school classes in session during part of it, the teachers involved will either work as a team with some of them free for morning worship each Sunday or teach only one half the year. This plan may assure them of continuous education in all the fields except psychology and teaching methods. These may be offered in monthly teachers' meetings, in the form of a course, or the insights and ideas may be communicated as the experienced teachers discuss their work with the newer ones. In larger churches this will be done by departments, with at least quarterly previewing and planning of lessons. Sometimes the parents are invited to these meetings since they are very much involved in the teaching, or should be. Often the parents in attendance gain confidence and are volunteers for future teaching assignments.

In a number of churches new teachers or prospects for the work are invited to observe a veteran for several weeks and to discuss the experience. Then the learner teaches for several weeks under observation, with evaluation following. Churches that feel this is not good for pupils often use recordings for the same purposes, and even veteran teachers benefit from listening to themselves in action. Many churches supply teachers with books and magazines in addition to curriculum materials, and arrange periodic briefings by the resources and techniques committee.

e. *Resources and techniques* for Christian education may be used with imagination and effect, but first they must be available. *The church library* need not be large, but it should have enthusiastic librarians, and budget enough to provide necessary volumes and place them in a setting that is attractive. The shelves may be kept fresh in appearance if the librarians will occasionally secure new dust jackets available from publishers, and will cover these with plastic material. Accessibility is more important than reading space, as the books will usually be read elsewhere. A librarian will be on duty Sunday morning, except during church. A self-service check-out system may be used during the week. The goal is *use* of books. The public library will provide a box of books for loan when the church librarians decide to feature a shelf on a particular subject or a group in the church desires to study a theme. Denominational boards and seminaries will suggest books for libraries of various sizes to be reviewed by the library committee before the annual budgeting of purchases, which may then be scheduled quarterly or monthly.

Paperback books, pamphlets, devotional guides, and tracts may be offered for sale or free distribution in vestibule and hall racks. A coin box will usually receive enough to pay for the enterprise. The Christian message reaches many people in this way. Thousands of small books are sold every week, and your denomination will suggest a variety of materials.

Audio-visual materials should not be substitutes for good program-planning and teaching, but may supplement and support the personal effort of good leaders. A church will want a tape recorder for use in training and teaching sessions, a slide projector, and a 16mm. motion picture projector. These may, of course, be borrowed from the local office of the denomination or council of churches. A rental agency may supply them, though the rental cost is often higher than the purchase price in the long run, the equipment inaccessible part of the time, and sometimes not in the best condition. Slides and films should usually be borrowed or rented. Sources will be the denomination, the council of churches, the public library, and rental agencies. Mail catalogs are available for churches that must order from agencies at a distance. Equipment should be locked up and available only to approved operators on written requisition.

Even more important than machines and materials is a group trained in their use and prepared to teach others who may wish to use them. Previews of films to be projected are essential, and machines should be tested just before use. Spare light bulbs and fuses should always be on hand. Prospective users should be encouraged to plan well in advance. While "any film may do" to fill an emergency, this practice soon places audio-visuals in disrepute. Church school departments, adult and youth groups, should plan their use of these materials for a year at a time, with catalogs and curriculum recommendations before them. Church groups should experiment with audio-visual materials. Some have developed effective presentations by taking 2″ x 2″ color slide pictures with an ordinary camera and projecting them, with an accompanying script and music recorded on a tape. Others are using the comparatively inexpensive sound-motion picture cameras to produce Bible stories and other features for projection. The learning involved in these processes is enthusiastic, rapid, and lasting in effect. Groups of churches are sponsoring early morning classes on television or radio and offering to supply a syllabus and bibliography — and, sometimes, even to mark papers.

Experimentation with teaching machines is in order. The key to success with these is good programming of material, a difficult and time-consuming process, but the results in prospect are worth the effort. A number of teachers are using flannel boards and turnover charts, as well as the rather expensive ballopticans, which project images on a large screen from any written or printed material and pictures. Closed-circuit television has been tried instead of building large department rooms. A master-teacher speaks to all classes in a department, with class discussion following.

f. *Conferences and camps* are important centers for communicating Christian attitudes and information. Churches cooperate in owning or renting and operating these centers, largely through denominational units. Larger churches may have their own centers, as well. Many of our Lord's most devoted servants made crucial decisions at a gathering of this kind.

Conferences may be conducted for a week at a time in the summer and for weekends the rest of the year. Accommodations range from primitive tent villages to " room and bath " facilities rented from an educational institution, but are usually in cabins sleeping eight and a counselor, or in dormitories. Conferences, with mornings and evenings devoted to serious subjects, and afternoons for recreation, are held for various age groups. There are many family camps with some programs for the whole group and some age-group activities. Camps with heavy emphasis on recreation are held for junior boys and girls and sometimes for junior high youth. Guidance for camp and conference committees is available from denominational leaders. National and area conferences and training schools are conducted under denominational and council of churches leadership for men and women and young people. Investment by the church in scholarships for these is usually sound. The delegates return to their local work with enthusiasm and a fresh viewpoint.

6. The Arts

The arts may have a place in the life of any congregation. A sound program will develop ways in which people with artistic gifts may be encouraged to express Christian faith through their creations, enriching the life of the church. Projects may include exhibitions, concerts of sacred music, writing contests, drama and poetry readings, plays, and lessons in the fine arts.

a. *Religious arts festivals* are conducted annually in a number of churches. Entries are invited in painting, graphic arts, sculpture, photographic still pictures and slides, poetry, drama, and music. Some festivals receive hundreds of entries. The prizes are modest, but sales often bring the artists a good return. The showing may continue afternoons and evenings for a week to ten days, with an award dinner at the beginning, and dramas, concerts, and other events, evenings. Two hundred members work on one festival that has about a thousand entries. A small one could be handled by twenty persons. Continued interest follows those festivals which are extremely selective and exhibit at most only the best third of the entries, returning the others before the showing with an expression of appreciation for the effort involved. An important result is new attention to the thought and life of the church by creative people. Another is growth beyond the mediocre and sentimental on the part of church people. This leads to use of fine, contemporary art, music, and poetry in the church, which in turn impresses upon able young people the freshness and vitality of the church.

b. *Children's religious arts festivals* are likely to follow those held by their elders. In one church even the primary children show paintings and sculpture, and one of their pictures is chosen each year for the cover of the church calendar on Children's Day. With the aid of a public school musician, the primary children also compose first the words and then the tune for a Children's Day hymn.

CHAPTER X

Witness

Witness is an integral part of the new life that springs up in response to God's redemptive acts of love in Jesus Christ. The church cannot ask whether it will witness any more than a tree can decide whether it will bear fruit. "Ye are the light of the world," Jesus tells his disciples; "let your light . . . shine." This is at once a statement of fact and a command. If it were not for the fact, the command would be a painful mockery. Because he has given them new life, he can promise, "Ye shall be witnesses unto me." The true church will witness; there is no question about this. The question for each generation concerns the forms of witness.

1. EVANGELISM

Jesus commissions his followers to "make disciples." He says they will be "fishers of men." He sees a great harvest waiting and few laborers, and urges prayer for laborers to enter into the harvest. He sends the Twelve and the Seventy on missions, and he continues to design projects in evangelism through the church in our time.

a. *Personal evangelism* involves the direct approach of one individual to another, and was a favorite method of our Savior. Each person who accepts Christ and becomes a part of his body obligates himself to this undertaking, and the church may not let him forget it. He will be expected always to be working with at least one person, and from time to time the church may help him with literature or meetings to which he may bring his friend. But, he is more likely to be aware of his obligation and be more effective if his efforts are part of a program.

b. *A program of visitation evangelism* includes a number of activities.

(1) *Finding prospects* is the first. Sources will include *guests* at church. In response to an invitation during the service they may sign cards available in pew racks and place them in the offering plate. Some churches ask the whole congregation to sign cards at Communion services and on Sundays during Advent and Lent. Aside from values to the membership this assures cards from many visitors. The cards usually have places for name and address and phone number, as well as a line indicating the place of church membership. Sometimes one may indicate a desire for a call or for uniting with the church.

The ritual of friendship is a variation of this plan. Churches use a 6″ x 9″ clipboard, often covered with leatherette, on which is mounted a fresh 5½″ x 8½″ sheet of ruled paper with three columns: Name, Address, Member or Guest. One of these is placed in each pew at the aisle. At the time of the ritual of friendship, the pastor asks that each person sign the sheet and pass it to his neighbor. When all in the pew have signed, it is passed back to the aisle and left there to be collected after the service. In passing it back, each person may note the names of others in the pew and be prepared for conversation after service. There are enthusiastic advocates of this plan, while others feel it is artificial or intrusive on worship.

Guest books in the vestibule may be helpful. More people will sign if there are members assigned to welcome guests before and after the service. They may lead them to the books. Sometimes the pastor, greeting folk at the door after the service, asks newcomers to sign the guest book. A secretary, often a volunteer, may stand near the pastor at the door after the service and record information he secures. One resourceful man uses an intercom with his secretary at the other end! Some prefer to hand cards to persons who give them information and ask them to write it down. A fortunate few may be able to rely entirely on memory.

Families enrolling members in the church school or other church groups are immediately reported to those in charge of evangelism. Other sources are suggestions from members and friends of the church, or referrals from out-of-town churches.

Newcomers are noted by members who see moving vans, observe a new man at work, or meet a child new at school. Names may also be secured from business or utility lists, or from agencies such as the Welcome Wagon.

Canvasses or surveys may be undertaken. A map of the area is secured. Handbills explaining the plan are distributed in advance. The visits are made by carefully trained visitors using a standard church survey card which may be obtained in quantity from denominational sources or the National Council of Churches. Call-backs are made if people are not at home the first time. The visitors are not to record information from neighbors, though they may express appreciation for it. It is frequently incorrect and based on guesses. Telephone calls are sometimes used in place of visits or preliminary to them in settled areas, when a Telekey type of directory is available. Telephone canvassing is easier but less likely to develop a maximum number of prospects. When a large area is to be surveyed, the church will wish to secure the cooperation of other churches, possibly through the council of churches.

(2) *Letters* will be sent to prospects by the pastor with the help of a group. They may be form letters, individually typed and personally signed. On Mondays a word of welcome and an invitation to return may be mailed to guests and to families with someone newly enrolled in activities. When names come in through suggestions, lists, or surveys, letters of welcome will be sent at once. Quarterly mailings of some sort will be sent all prospects, as well as notices for special services and events. Some churches send the weekly newsletter.

(3) *Files* will include all prospects. As a name is secured, it may be checked against the file and entered if it is not there. As information comes in, it will be added. The cards may be filed alphabetically and will be a different color from those of members. In larger churches it may be helpful to use church district numbers and to have one file of prospects by districts. When there is a large file, it may be wise to tab and mark cards as the names are referred to various persons for calling. Some files have a duplicate card which " travels " with telephoners and callers. Cards representing persons who are guests often, but are not prospects for membership, may be placed in a separate " Guests " section for reference. New names are regu-

larly checked against this section as well as the other, so that embarrassing mistakes are avoided.

(4) *Calling procedures* for dealing with prospects may differ in view of the church location, the age of the community, and the personnel available. A women's telephone group may receive new names about which little is known. Each name is entered on a reply card which is to be returned within a week. The call is to extend a welcome and elicit information. An invitation committee composed of men may then undertake visits, two by two. Often this group meets weekly or monthly for luncheon or dinner, or in the early evening, with programs for training and reports. Visits may follow the meetings. After getting acquainted with prospects, the men talk of their own experiences as Christians. Some have a mimeographed or printed leaflet which they place in the hands of new friends and read aloud with comments. If the atmosphere seems favorable, they then invite a decision for Christ and his church which may be recorded on a decision card. A record of the call, with information, is returned on an assignment slip and entered on the file card. The pastor calls as soon as he can. Further calls are made periodically by the invitation committee or the pastor or by individuals or couples chosen by them until there is a decision.

(5) *An annual evangelistic visitation* should supplement the week-by-week effort. Ten percent of the congregation should be enrolled and trained as visitors. They ought to understand exactly what they are going to do and why. Other members of the church may be enlisted to pray for the effort. Following a service of dedication on a Sunday morning, and a luncheon at the church, the visitors will go out. An experienced person will be sent with each new recruit. The entire prospect list will be visited. When enough visitors are available, there may be a canvass of some residential streets or apartments. If this is done by plan on a five-year cycle — with preference each year to new developments — information on the whole area may be kept up to date. Visitors going to persons on the prospect list will be trained to follow the approach of the invitation committee. Those who canvass should be prepared to express the interest of the congregation, and elicit information, and make friends. Where there are openings they may offer to drive new friends

to church the following Sunday, or to return for another call.

c. *An inquirers' class* may meet regularly, offering instruction in Christian theology and practice. The time may be the church school hour on Sunday morning, a Sunday afternoon, or an evening during the week. The period is rarely less than three weeks and in a few churches extends over two years. Attendance does not imply an obligation to unite with the church, but is generally required of those who would become communicants. The group is sometimes called a confirmation class or a communicants class. A few churches require extensive reading and an examination. Usually there is a separate class for boys and girls who are about to be received as communicants, and it will have not less than twelve sessions.

d. *Preaching missions* may be planned for one night a week during Lent or in the fall, with a succession of guest preachers. An alternative is a series with one guest preacher beginning on one Sunday and running through another, with services on a number of week-nights in between. Sometimes a group of churches cooperate in a large venture. Whatever the plan, it will be effective only if accompanied by a program of personal evangelism.

e. *New possibilities* include radio and television programs, lunch hour or evening meetings at the church or in a restaurant for business people, in a plant for industrial workers, on a public square or shopping plaza for people of all sorts, in a coffee shop for the avant-garde. Experiments are in progress with residential centers attached to campus churches. It would be interesting to see what would happen if a church opened a residential center for unmarried industrial workers across from a large factory. The center could have a twenty-four-hour program for shift workers, with a library and reading room, Bible classes, and recreation rooms. Reading rooms could be effective in busy downtown locations and large shopping plazas. Classified advertising in the "personals" section of newspapers, used effectively in Japan, may have possibilities in America.

f. *Assimilation* is an important sequel to the evangelistic effort and may be considered a part of it. A person who accepts Christ but does not become a functioning part of his body will eventually have a withered faith.

One pattern for assimilation involves five steps: (1) Reception into membership is arranged in such a way as to emphasize its importance. The process of reception by the official board and the congregation is carefully planned and carried forward with dignity. The new members are greeted in a receiving line after the service. Sometimes, and especially in the case of a youth class, a dinner is given in their honor. (2) An officer invites them to an informal evening in a home, where group representatives tell of activities and a succession of slides depicts the program of the church. Friendship with church leaders begins to develop during the refreshment period. Sometimes the new group elects a chairman who will convene them occasionally during the first year. (3) An officer calls, presenting a booklet entitled *Your Church and Your Life*. It outlines the church program, explains the services available in times of need, and suggests forms of service. This may be discussed. The officer makes mental notes of interest and later telephones representatives of appropriate groups. He requests that the new person be invited to group meetings by someone who will accompany him the first time. (4) A booklet on finances is mailed. It is followed within a week by a member of the stewardship commission. The booklet describes the church property and the capital investment of the entire communion all over the world in which the new member has a part ownership. The local and world budget is explained. The system of proportionate giving is discussed, with explanations of contributions which may be requested over and above the weekly amount pledged. Since the new member has read the booklet before the arrival of the visitor and now has his questions answered, he is asked to make a weekly pledge for the remainder of the year. (5) The pastor calls on the new family within the first few months. He may wish to arrange informally for other calls by members, or to ask the newcomers to make a call or two. When they begin to serve, assimilation is well under way.

2. World Mission

World mission is a continuation of evangelism beyond the local situation. If it is to fulfill the Lord's commission, the congregation must be involved in the work of the whole church wherever it may be.

a. *Personal interest* and mutual concern will develop as the people of a church meet Christians from other parts of their own country and the wide world. Missionaries or fraternal workers and leaders who have grown up in churches continents away may be invited to speak and spend time in a local church. There may be a week of mission or an ecumenical weekend with several visitors from national missions and overseas churches. One church builds full-sized scenes from half a dozen areas each year to give the occasion colorful appeal. Features include prayer meetings, lectures, slides and motion pictures, children's folk games and dances, a play, recordings of music, printed materials, maps, dinners with exotic foods, and small gatherings in homes where the visitors are entertained. The event gives focus to a program and requires extensive research and ecumenical correspondence during the year by a number of groups.

A church may, through denominational channels, arrange for the full or partial support of missionaries or fraternal workers or national church leaders in several parts of the world. Sometimes it is possible to arrange for these persons to stay in the community and be a part of the church's life during a furlough or visit. Churches near educational institutions or medical centers may have a member who will give a furnished house to be a furlough home, ensuring a different family from overseas in residence each year. In any event, there may be correspondence and an exchange of pictures. Overseas students in attendance at nearby schools may be entertained at the church and in homes of the congregation. If possible, some of them are encouraged to be a part of the church family while in residence. The church may participate in a student exchange program or have a number of its families do so.

Study projects may include mission themes and subjects of ecumenical concern. A *Year Book of Prayer for Missions,* with a listing of all mission enterprises and the persons involved, may be used in the homes of the congregation. Reports of mission activity may be made from time to time in services. Church publications may carry word from workers in other places and description of mission enterprises. Literature may be placed in vestibules and halls and distributed through groups. There may be a mission center in the hall with a large world map. This will show particular interests with colored pins and ribbons. It may have posted, under or beside it, recent pictures and letters.

Members may be encouraged to visit the church at work whenever they go on business or pleasure trips. Occasions for reports and showing of pictures will spread enthusiasm and increase participation. Youth groups may plan annual trips by bus to churches doing effective work in difficult or unusual circumstances. People going distances or overseas may be furnished with contacts and publicly commissioned before they go. Students may be encouraged to join summer caravans for work in mission areas of America, or financially helped to participate in overseas work camps.

b. *Recruits* for short-term service or summer work may be secured. Often there is need for teachers, physicians, surgeons, dentists, administrators, construction specialists, and others. One church may have volunteers on assignments varying from a few weeks to several years. The individuals pay their own way, or their travel costs are borne by their church with the field covering local expenses. Services of this sort are especially attractive to youth and retired persons, though more than one busy doctor gives a month or two every few years.

Lifetime workers may be enlisted, supported in securing the necessary education and encouraged by the prayers and gifts of groups in the church. An enlistment program should be carefully planned and carried forward. Without pressure the most capable youth in the church are made aware of needs for ministers, Christian educators, and missionaries of all sorts. A scholarship fund may be maintained. Students preparing for these vocations are frequently brought to the church, and meet with the young people.

c. *Financial participation* in the world mission should be substantial. There will be continual examination of the church's stewardship in this respect, with plans for increasing participation. In addition to a solid part of the pledged income, there may be group gifts and some special offerings. One church has opportunity offerings once a month for special mission causes. Other churches feel it is better to work steadily toward increased pledges and equal budgets for local expenses and the world mission.

d. *Denominational relationships* may be cultivated so that members are aware of the larger communion of which the congregation is a part. Representatives will be carefully chosen for area and national deliberative bodies, for training sessions and promotional gatherings. Efforts will be made to have members serving on area and national boards and committees. Subscriptions to denominational magazines may be encouraged and the extensive literature commended to groups. Members may be encouraged to help in special projects at other churches and missions, and in camps, conference centers, hospitals, and homes.

e. *Interdenominational relationships,* particularly with respect to councils of churches, may be approached in the same manner. Local and state councils are usually important to the mission of the church in developing a total strategy and comity arrangements for all the churches, which avoid needless waste. They function effectively in joint leadership education projects, community surveys, radio and television programming, and the development of coordinated activity in rural areas or the inner city. They offer opportunities for wide Christian fellowship and provide a united voice for Protestantism when issues arise on which all are agreed.

f. *Ecumenical relationships* and opportunities to perform services no communion can offer alone, such as care for refugees and relief of hunger and distress, as well as meetings in which the church is drawn nearer to unity, are provided by the National Council of Churches and the World Council.

3. Stewardship

Stewardship is an indispensable element in witness. Every Christian is under obligation to place himself and all that he possesses at his Lord's disposal. The church program may provide for a year-round effort to make everyone aware of his responsibility. There will be references in sermons and lessons. Printed materials in abundance cover all aspects of stewardship. They may be used for group programs or placed in the hands of individuals.

a. *Christian vocation* will be stressed, with efforts to understand its implications for workaday life. Members engaged in a particular kind of work may gather once or regularly for a time to determine if they care about what it means to serve Christ as a bricklayer or a doctor, a machine operator or a homemaker. Occasionally in other groups or conferences an attempt will be made to discuss the implications of the idea that each Christian has a calling. This may raise some painful, but important, questions about particular jobs and practices in business and industry. It may lead to some changes in employment and some innovations in offices and shops.

b. *Calls to avocational activities* may be considered by officers and groups. It may be assumed that every Christian will have some gifts that should be put to work for the good of the whole church or community. Guidelines may be worked out concerning the allocation of leisure to church activities, community service, home duties, recreation, and rest. A personnel program related to this is discussed in Chapter V.

c. *Christian family life* may be explored. Groups may study the meaning of sex, the development of healthy and Christian attitudes before marriage and afterward, the sharing of tasks within the home and authority relationships there, the ethics of planned parenthood, and relations between parents and children at various stages of life.

d. *The use of money* will be subjected to study and discussion. Ways will be found to have as many members as possible consider how much a Christian should spend on himself and to what extent there should be austerity or even self-denial. Further attention may be given to savings and insurance, budgets and disciplined spending, circumstances justifying debts and installment buying.

e. *Giving* will be discussed. Should one give a definite percentage of income, such as the tithe, or 10 percent? Should the percentage be graduated in relation to the size of income or family obligations? Should Christians keep an amount equal to a national average of some sort or a group average and give away all the rest? How much should be given through the church and how much through community agencies or to individuals? Most Christians now give about 2 percent of income to the church. A number of churches have decided that members will be urged gradually to work toward a minimum pledge of 5 percent to the church with the other 5 percent of the tithe used for community agencies, individual charities, special offerings, and support of church organizations.

f. *An annual Every Member Canvass* is conducted in most churches, and is usually planned for the second Sunday in November. This is known as Stewardship Sunday, and is cleared of other emphases by national agreement. The Religion In American Life committee offers free help in preparation for this day with special billboard advertisements and programs on radio and television networks.

The canvass frequently involves visits to each home by two representatives of the church who ask for a pledge toward the work of the congregation which will be given week by week throughout the year. A popular variation is reception of pledges at the conclusion of a service of worship, with visits in the afternoon to homes not represented in church. A few congregations depend on a mail canvass, which never results in maximum giving. Whether every home is visited or most pledges are received in church, extensive preparations are necessary. The stewardship commission should appoint a canvass committee at the beginning of each year, and plans for November should be ready by March.

A minimum organization for an effective canvass will include a general chairman and subcommittees on personnel, letters and literature, training, program, arrangements, and auditing. The personnel committee should have a captain for every four teams of canvassers, a section leader for every five captains, and a division leader for every five section leaders. If every home is to be visited in one afternoon and evening by a team of two members, each from a different home, no team should be assigned to more than five homes, in addition to the two homes represented in the team. If the pledges are to be received in church, with visits only to absentees, one may assume that about half the pledges will be made in church for about 80 percent of the total amount that will be pledged, and only half as many teams will be needed as for a canvass of every home. This assumes that a real effort will be made to have members in church, through announcements, letters, telephone calls, and in some years through preliminary visits by canvassers. Sometimes each team is assigned five active families and five less likely to be active. The teams telephone all the families before Stewardship Sunday in an effort to persuade as many as possible to attend.

The personnel committee recruits canvassers step by step. Following an estimate of the number of calls to be made, a list of possible workers is prepared. It should have twice as many prospects as will be needed. In May the division chairmen should be appointed and they should have their section leaders by early June. The section leaders may then be given lists of ten persons each. From these they are expected to secure five captains by the end of June. At this time a letter may be sent to the persons on the prospective list of canvassers, indicating the dates of the canvass and the hope they will be willing to serve when asked in the fall. Early in September the captains meet and each receives a list of twenty names, from which he is expected to enlist ten to complete his five teams by October 15.

During the summer the auditing committee prepares duplicate canvass cards for each family in the church. Information noted includes the family name, and the first names of members, with such other data as may be useful. These cards are sorted geographically and assigned to teams. After the team number is placed on both cards one of them is removed and placed in an alphabetical file to be retained by the committee. The other is given to the team about two weeks before canvass time through the divisional organization. If there is a worship type of canvass, the auditing committee goes to work immediately after church. A card is pulled from the alphabet file for every pledge card turned in at the service. These cards of persons who have pledged are sorted by team number and given to the teams through the divisional organization with instructions to remove their duplicates from the cards assigned to the team.

The arrangements committee is responsible for meals and meetings, the program committee for the features of these occasions and the promotion of attendance, the committee on letters and literature cooperates with these committees and sends at least one letter to the congregation before the canvass. A brochure may be included in this mailing. It will tell the story of the church's work at home and abroad. A budget for the coming year may be included, or the budget of the current year may be noted, with the suggestion that expenditures for the year ahead will depend on the giving. Often there is a dinner or a series of dinners for the congregation the week before the canvass with a presentation of the budget and a program setting forth the importance of the work to be done. Luncheon may be served to the canvassers before they go out after church. This offers a period for instruction.

The program should be carefully prepared by the training committee. There may be motion pictures or slides showing methods, or this may be done in a series of skits by members. If there has been a worship canvass, the results may be announced. The assignments are distributed. The canvassers go out. When families are not at home, a brightly colored notice is left between the doorknob and doorjamb. It says the canvassers were sorry to miss these folks and will return. After their other calls, they pass that house. If the notice is gone, the family has probably returned and a call may be made. If it is there, the visitors go home but allow time on their evening journey to the report meeting for a trip past the house in the hope the notice will be gone. Reports are received and tabulated and arrangements made for later call-backs at a meeting in the church about seven thirty P.M. or earlier if there is an eight o'clock service. Teams will make more call-backs on Sunday if no reports are received until early evening. Some churches have special teams for call-backs after Sunday, composed of those who cannot serve on Sunday afternoons.

g. *A Christian will* may be discussed in church groups and suggested in publications as a means of extending one's service to Christ. Many whose resources are limited in life may be able to leave substantial amounts for Christian work. Denominational literature is available on this, as on most aspects of stewardship.

4. Church and Society

Social education and action is a natural outcome of Christian experience and will have a place in the church program.

a. *The social and economic welfare* of individuals and families in the congregation and community will be a concern. The church will have some funds for the relief of financial distress and will work closely with community agencies in the field, supplementing their efforts when needs arise suddenly or are not covered by provisions of law. The church may also deal with situations of no interest to the agencies, such as the instance of a member who must travel a long distance for special medical treatment. Vocational counseling may be offered by a group of retired men who may also help persons find jobs. If there is no homemakers' service in the community, a group of church women may start one in connection with a Family Service agency, or operate a modest plan as a church service. This involves "substitute homemakers" who go in for a day at a time when a mother is ill. The men of the church may support an existing Big Brother agency or in its absence, organize one under church or Community Chest auspices. Under this plan a man agrees to be a particular friend of a youth who has shown the first signs of delinquency or has had a brush with the law. A youth canteen may be operated by the church one evening or several evenings a week. Variations include athletic teams in season, boys' clubs, girls' clubs, Scout troops, Brownies, Cubs, Campfire Girls, summer camps, and day camps. Mothers' clubs may raise the sights of women in a depressed neighborhood, or provide a creative fellowship and counseling service for young mothers. Day nurseries may provide for children of working mothers. Golden age clubs may offer a variety of interests for older people in a community and even provide "clubhouse" facilities every day for lonely people. The church may pioneer in some of these areas, passing the established activity on to community sponsorship after a time.

There may be a plan to prepare members for effective service in community agencies. Participation may be encouraged in such organizations as the Community Chest, the Y.M.C.A., the Y.W.C.A., Family Service, Planned Parenthood, the NAACP, the Boy Scouts, the Girl Scouts, the P.T.A., the Health Association and its constituent groups, the American Red Cross and its Gray Ladies service, Alcoholics Anonymous, the Boys' Clubs of America, and the boards of hospitals. Membership in service clubs, business and professional organizations, unions and employers' associations, may be presented as opportunities for Christian witness and social progress.

A church group may call attention to the need for community interest and action for the welfare of school dropouts, or new ethnic groups moving into the community, or prisoners, or migrant workers. They may take a part in organizing groups to meet special needs. The people of one church became so concerned about migrants in camps outside their city that they organized a task force of eighty workers, including schoolteachers, physicians, nurses, youth with skill at games, and women who could teach cooking and sewing. A car dealer loaned a station wagon; a sewing machine company gave several machines. A motion-picture projector was secured. Lessons and services of all sorts were offered in the camps, including reading, medical and legal advice, hygiene, planned parenthood, and vocational training—as well as services of worship, Christian education, and entertainment. The following year the council of churches took responsibility and enlarged the work with the aid of many churches.

A men's group became concerned about prisoners in their city. They visited jails and talked with persons in authority. They offered help in developing community attitudes, in improved food service, in recreational facilities, in sponsorship of parolees. The fact of their interest and their frequent visits raised the sights of employees and brought about improvements. They joined with officials in seeking legislation to make the penal system a force for rehabilitation rather than a necessary evil. Groups of churchmen in Louisville, Kentucky, have worked in this manner in connection with prisons, county hospitals, police stations, institutions for mentally deficient or emotionally disturbed persons, courts, and detention centers for delinquent children. A couples group in a small city wrote to a large city newspaper offering to entertain children from the city streets in their homes for two weeks at a time. In the course of five years they have enlisted other couples and now care for hundreds of children every summer.

Groups of women weekly prepare tens of thousands of bandages for hospitals at home and abroad, and sew articles such as layettes and clothing. Others, often with the help of men's groups for packing, collect and send overseas unnumbered tons of clean, used clothing. Many churches have regularly scheduled fall and spring collections of clothing for this purpose. Others have Good-as-New sales of used clothing that offer a way to secure quality garments at reasonable prices. This is especially helpful to families with a number of small children. The rummage sale is still used as a fund-raising device in many churches. It would be interesting to see what could be done if women from a group of churches rented a store in a depressed section on a permanent basis, fitted it up nicely for sales, and installed a coffee area and club facilities. It should pay for itself and perform evangelistic and social functions.

A men's group may study the use of beverage alcohol, using literature available from the denomination. They may issue booklets on the subject for teen-agers and parents. They may start community action to open a nonalcoholic night club for young people, with a program good enough to compete with commercial enterprises that sell liquor. They may work in a center for the treatment of alcoholics, with a halfway house as a residence for men who have been down and are coming back to normal life. They may support or start a mission or service center for homeless men. They may sponsor an advertising campaign against drinking before driving. All these things may be better done through the establishment of a community committee on alcohol or a branch of Allied Forces, Inc. Whatever may be done, it is worthwhile to work with Alcoholics Anonymous, and perhaps to offer a meeting room at the church to at least one AA group.

The church may have a plan for encouraging some members to seek careers in politics. Certainly the program should be designed to overcome the unrealistic perfectionism that will have nothing to do with the political arena because it involves compromise.

b. *A program of action* is likely to emerge only after an educational program, and it must constantly be undergirded by research if it is to deal effectively with delicate issues. Since action is often the best form of education, this field requires a good blend of study and activity. For example, a small group may be concerned about racial integration in the church and community. After a period of study and discussion, they may suggest to the minister that more sermon references to the subject may be in order. He may arrange pulpit exchanges with able Negro preachers. The process of exchange may lead to some visiting between congregations even if they are in different cities. Educational programs about racial problems and the roots of prejudice may be offered to church groups. Literature may be available and brief articles may be written for the church's weekly paper or calendar. The official board may make the building available to Negro or other minority groups for special services or meetings, and may suggest an open housing covenant for signature by members. Members may be encouraged to serve in community groups sponsored by a human relations commission. They may start a commission, if there is none, to deal with desirable advances and the emergency stresses that develop along with progress. When Negroes attend church or move into the community they may, for a time, receive priority in evangelistic effort. As they unite with the church, they may be encouraged, as they are able, to volunteer for the choir, for teaching classes, and for service that will prepare for membership in boards. An effective program will be a blend of education and action.

c. *The first step in social education and action* may be formation of a concerned group to study some of the things we have discussed, as well as community issues like good housing, economic issues like full employment, church and state issues like support of parochial schools, and international issues like peace and disarmament. Through their discussions individuals in the group who may be in the official board, or have other associations, may be led to propose further study and research in different groups and some action projects. Denominational and ecumenical pronouncements and literature may be used to good effect in this process.

5. Public Relations

Public relations activities include use of newspapers, printed and duplicated materials, and radio or television announcements and programs.

a. *The public image of a congregation* will depend on what it does. No amount of cleverness in handling publicity will help very much if the program is inadequate. Services of worship in which persons find themselves face-to-face with God, preaching through which God speaks, nurture that helps people grow, witness that results in readiness for changes God can effect in individuals and society — these evidences of vital life cannot be hidden. It is possible, by publicity, to reach some people who would not otherwise know of the church, and to attract some of them who may then feel the impact of its life and work.

b. *Newspapers* are read by almost everyone. It is surprising how many people can tell you about something noted briefly in an obscure corner of newsprint. News stories receive more attention than notices or advertisements. The congregation may have an individual or group that will take responsibility for regular releases to the newspaper, or the pastor may do this. Whoever prepares stories is well advised first to become acquainted with the people at the paper. He will discover something of the pressures under which they operate: the competition for limited space, the deadlines beyond which nothing can be printed, the lurking danger of serious errors. He will feel something of their passion for the truth, their insatiable hunger for facts, their impatience toward misrepresentation, their low threshold for boredom, and high resistance to enthusiasm. He will also be impressed with their sense of responsibility to the community and their willingness to help in a good cause. He will learn when feature articles are written and how easily they may lose their places if something more newsworthy comes along, or a large advertisement preempts space. Other facts of importance are the hours a photographer may be made available and how much in advance of publication pictures must be taken; the deadlines for news copy in a morning or evening paper, the proper person to receive material, and when he may be reached. If there are two papers, the first release on big stories may be alternated between them. When the same event is described for both, it should be with different emphases.

The copy, double-spaced on 8½″ x 11″ paper, will answer Kipling's questions:

> "What and Why and When
> And How and Where and Who."

The important information will come first, and the whole will be checked for accuracy and spelling. Careful observance of the fate of material and some discussion with friends at the paper will enable the writer to improve copy. Stories should be submitted only if the writer can affirm, " I would read this if it concerned a group in which I have no present interest." News has public interest and this is rarely true of sermon topics or notices of regular events at the church. It may be true of church elections, staff changes, building projects, financial campaigns, anniversary celebrations, statistics of growth, guest speakers, new departures and experiments in nurture and witness, festivals, statements and projects in the field of social action. News must be current, or it is dead. Material on a big event should not be released too soon or it is forgotten before the occasion. Often people at the paper will help in designing a release schedule, with a succession of features, for something like a week of mission or a one hundredth anniversary.

c. *Advertisements* may serve a church in one of two ways: (1) A notice on the Saturday church page records the fact of its existence and may give an impression of vitality. This is usually a waste of money for a neighborhood church, but may be one of a few ways the downtown church reaches potential members. Sermon titles should be included only if they are specifically designed to interest outsiders. The dreary topics usually found in this connection give a most unfortunate impression of what goes on in church. (2) The church page, or another part of the paper, may be an excellent place to spend money when opening a new program of general interest or introducing an outstanding speaker. Type and format should be varied so that the advertisement stands out. Constant study of vogues in print and arrangement on the church page will enable one to devise something different.

d. *The church bulletin* may have public relations values. Its appearance creates an impression favorable or unfavorable to the church. It may be better to have no bulletin if it is not possible to produce one that is attractive. Some churches mail bulletins to the homes of members and prospects in advance of services and place copies on the key desks at hotels. Others use the bulletin only for the order of service and the listing of officers and stated meetings. A separate weekly or monthly publication carrying news and notices is mailed and distributed after church and in public places. This removes the temptation to read news during worship, and may cost no more if the bulletin and " the news " are each limited to two sides of a small sheet.

e. *The church news,* which may be given a suitable name, can, if it is printed, be entered as second-class matter for weekly mailing. This results in a very small cost for postage. The front page will feature the most important events of the week at the church. There may be a brief devotional article and suggested daily Bible readings. A calendar for the coming week is useful. Groups wishing to have notices included must observe a deadline that is often ten days before publication. One thing most people will read is the letter from the pastor, which may be so designed that it seems like a personal visit each week. It is better to leave general material to denominational magazines. A single pertinent sheet is preferable to a commercial publication that allows the local church a few pages and contains pages of fill. Pictures of persons and events in the church and line cuts that do not reek of yesterday may improve the paper, but they are expensive.

f. *Publications* may be produced by a stencil process, letterpress, or offset. Most church bulletins and many weekly papers are mimeographed. The stencil process has been greatly improved and a good operator may produce beautiful work. Its major disadvantage is its exclusion from second-class mailing privileges. Justifying, or bringing the right-hand margin to a straight line, will improve appearance. The rough copy is typed up to, or somewhat short of, a perpendicular pencil line, and never beyond it. The space between short lines and the pencil line is filled with asterisks. The operator then goes over each line placing a pencil check at each point where a space is to be added to bring that line exactly to the right margin. Each line requires one check for each asterisk. The copy is then retyped.

Printing by letterpress is excellent when a church can afford the expense and when a printer can be found who has an aesthetic sense, a choice of up-to-date type, and a personal interest in doing a good job. Offset printing, which is a form of lithography, has the major advantage over printing that pictures and drawings may be inexpensively produced. When the work is done commercially, other costs are about the same as printing. However, office lithographs that can produce superb work are now available. If there is a church secretary with mechanical aptitude, a large church may save up to a third of the printing bill, even when amortization of equipment and labor costs are included. Copy is typed and justified on good white paper. A variable spacing typewriter with a carbon ribbon produces the finest appearance at a moderate cost. It is possible to secure machines that offer a choice of type and do their own justifying, but this is only practical when the annual printing budget is above three thousand dollars. Headlines may be set with " paper type," available commercially. This is pasted in position over the typed copy and allows for great variety. The material is then sent out to be professionally photographed, an inexpensive process. The negative comes back and is imposed on a sensitized copper plate that reacts to light. The plate is then mounted on the rotary lithograph machine which will produce a limitless number of copies. It is only fair to note that a lithograph is a much more complicated machine than a stencil duplicator, and some operators never master the art of producing good copy. Before making any purchase, a church should arrange for at least two persons from the staff to operate a demonstration machine.

g. *Radio and television* present opportunities for the local church. All churches may regularly send word of activities to stations and to particular programs that specialize in community announcements. As in the case of newspapers, there should be someone in the congregation who becomes acquainted with the broadcasting people, knows what each will use, and keeps him supplied with church news.

Services may be broadcast. The format of the average hour of worship does not make an ideal radio or television program and the lights necessary for television do not enhance a service in church. However, the regular radio broadcast of a service has the long-run effect of bringing many people to the church, and a televised service is followed by increased attendance. An occasional radio broadcast of a service, even in a monthly sequence arranged through a council of churches, has limited value since the quality is uneven and no consistent listening is developed. It does permit shut-in members to participate to some extent in the service at their own churches and it may reach some strangers. Regular preaching on the air can be very effective in reaching people with the gospel. Despite disclaimers, few developments to date have had the lasting popularity of such programs as Ralph Sockman's regular broadcast for more than twenty-five years, and that of "The Lutheran Hour." The local congregation may support national programs of this sort and of the more experimental variety. It may also arrange for a weekly fifteen-minute service primarily devoted to preaching. One downtown church receives members every year who first became interested through a weekly radio service. And each year the number of persons listening has grown. Another church, similarly situated, records the anthem and sermon for a half-hour Sunday evening broadcast which has had an important effect on that congregation's reputation and growth in difficult circumstances. Church programs featuring drama, music, reports of projects, panels, lectures, displays of art, and other possibilities may be worked out and offered to stations by a church or group of churches. There is a large field here for dedicated imagination and experimentation.

Chapter XI

Supporting Activities

Supporting activities are essential for worship, nurture, and witness. Buildings and finances, office procedures and housekeeping, are often given an exaggerated importance that justifies prophetic impatience. Idolatry in any form is bad, but if we are to get along without anything that can be idolized, life will be poor indeed. A more sensible course is to use the resources God places at our disposal for his work, never losing sight of their instrumental character, and consciously resisting the temptation to turn means into ends. The demands of the institution may be irksome, and even dangerous, but without it we cannot even deliver a cup of cold water to a brother across the seas, not to speak of weightier matters. Plainly, there must be supporting activities if the church is to fulfill its commission.

1. Buildings and Equipment

Buildings and equipment must be acquired and maintained. There must be a place for worship, space for fellowship and educational activities, and a center for witness. Few will be satisfied to offer God only the worship possible in a small room. The desire for majestic space and a great organ and choir will be understood by our Lord, who worshiped in the simplicity of the synagogue but also went up to the splendid Temple. Educational space may be limited in those few churches which are attempting to center the entire task of Christian nurture for children in the home, and therefore have no classes for boys and girls. Others that maintain classes for children and youth may scatter them through homes of the community. Usually this proves to be a temporary arrangement, inconvenient for families, and difficult to supervise. Christian witness goes on everywhere, but if it is to be coordinated and if more and more people are to work together, there must be a center with facilities for meetings and communication.

It is true that a disproportionate share of church income often goes into church buildings. The constantly changing residential patterns suggest that the ancient plan of building for the ages may be wasteful. Modern church buildings must be erected with awareness that they may be razed within forty to fifty years to make way for a road, a business block, or a housing project. In even less time the structure may require extensive changes to serve needs of different people. One solution is to use comparatively inexpensive materials and keep everything simple. This may be combined with limited space requirements based on a program of multiple services and several church school sessions. The money saved may be used to more effect in programs at home and abroad.

Whatever may be built will require maintenance. Some members will have to give attention to this. They may keep a Maintenance Plan Book with a page for each major area, such as the roof, the exterior pointing and paint, the windows, the heating and ventilating system, the wiring, the plumbing, and the decoration and furnishings of each room. They may work out a long-range plan for replacements and repairs, estimating the useful life of present materials. Added to this, on each page will be a record of repair, replacement, and improvement, with new estimates of life expectancy. On this basis it will be possible to budget intelligently and supervise effectively. Modest undertakings within the capacity of the custodian or groups of members may be planned for quiet seasons. The help of groups may be solicited well in advance. Anticipated purchases may be arranged at favorable prices. Members will learn that they do not need to withhold money from regular giving to be ready for emergency appeals.

Policies concerning the use of rooms and facilities may be determined and published or posted, together with a procedure by which groups are assigned space for regular or special meetings. Weekly and monthly work schedules should be prepared for the sexton and volunteers.

Fire prevention measures and safety provisions may be developed. This will include the marking of exits and posting in every room of a small map and instructions for emergency evacuation. Periodic inspection may eliminate unnoticed hazards. A consultation with ushers and church school leaders should result in detailed plans for emergencies, including safe removal of infants and small children. Fire drills may be held occasionally. An insurance program will cover fire and storm hazards and possible liabilities, including those incurred when members use their cars in any church service such as transportation of persons or equipment, or even the delivery of flowers to the sick. Frequent reviews will assure the program's adequacy.

2. Office Procedures and Arrangements

a. Filing is important; order is better than chaos. A church office should have clean desks. As the man with cluttered mind and desk performs one task, five others tug at his sleeve. Precious minutes go by as he tries to decide what comes next. He reads every letter and paper on the desk several times in the process of sorting files. Then, in all likelihood, he cannot find what he needs.

A clean desk saves time. Answer letters when you receive them. If this is impossible, place letters or papers in one of two folders in the file drawer of the desk. The tag on one folder reads " Correspondence." Try to keep it empty as much of the time as possible. The second folder bears the title " Correspondence B." Use it for letters and memos acknowledged, but unanswerable without further information, and for inquiries and assignments demanding large expenditures of time. A few words on the face of the folder or on the first sheet inside identify each paper within it. Cross these entries off and send the papers on their way as you complete the work related to them.

Mark papers for filing the first time you see them or as you take them out of the correspondence folders. Write the filing category in the upper left-hand corner and place them in a " Filing " folder in the file drawer of the desk. Empty this folder into the appropriate folders in the file at the first free moment. If you have a secretary, she will do this. When you have no appropriate folder for a letter or paper, make one. Do not waste time making up folders before you need them. If you have a very large file, you may wish to have a 3″ x 5″ file card index of file folder categories in your desk.

See that papers on the desk concern only the subject under consideration. File them when that piece of business gives way to another. This takes much less time than sorting things out periodically and hunting for lost items. Use the file drawer of the desk for the correspondence folders, the "Filing" folder, a folder of counseling records marked "Confidential," a transfer folder for papers you wish to take home, and a few folders dealing with current projects which go back to the main file when the work on them is completed. Use another drawer for stationery and supplies. Keep one drawer empty, except as you use it to clear the desk of working papers when you have an unexpected visitor. The clean desk emphasizes your intention to give him your full attention.

You may keep your engagement calendar on the desk, or you may prefer to use a top drawer for the flat 9″ x 12″ type which covers a month on each page. You may now secure small duplicates of this form for pocket use, but many ministers avoid the practice of making engagements on the basis of a pocket calendar. The habit of confirming engagements only from the desk calendar gives time for reflection and enables you to keep the whole month in balance. It is also the only way you can depend on a secretary to make office appointments and remind you of obligations. You may use an "Engagements" folder in which letters and replies dealing with commitments may be filed by date.

File sermons chronologically, using a folder for all the sermons of each year, dated and numbered. Discourses for 1965 may be numbered 6500 to 6599, those for 1966, 6600 to 6699. A desk folder marked "Sermons" is a good place for the annual planning sheets that list all the sermons for a year. This will be a convenient chronological index if the numbers are placed after the sermons. Eventually, you may want an alphabetical card index of sermon titles and a card index of texts filed by books of the Bible. Experience will indicate whether the two card files are worth the time invested in them. Make them only when you begin to have trouble locating sermons from the simple chronological index.

Few files of sermon materials are worth the time involved in maintaining them. Material you do not wish to file with one of the sermons under preparation may be placed in a "Sermon Materials" folder, where papers remain in chronological order as received. Use notes on the front of the folder to identify each item. Start a new folder when the last is filled. Throw out the older ones when you no longer refer to them. One of America's most famous preachers used this system, except that he filled a desk drawer with notes and clippings. When the drawer became crowded, he threw away the contents and started over! This was a recognition of the fact that sermons take shape in the mind and not in file drawers.

Cataloging books wastes time. Shelve them according to a few general categories, and follow an alphabetical arrangement of authors within the categories if you have time. Make notes in the backs of books as you read. You will know where to look when you need the material, or you can find it more quickly than you can develop an elaborate system.

b. In correspondence an immediate answer is the most appreciated, and it takes the least time. You can answer many letters with two or three lines in longhand on a letterhead. If you have a secretary, clip the reply to the original letter. She can note the answer on the original for the file and address an envelope for the reply. Most letters can be answered briefly, and should be. The ease of dictation tempts men to say too much. Dictating machines save time for both pastor and secretary and are well worth their cost. If you secure one that records for a half hour at a time, you may use it in church to take down sermons.

When originating correspondence, and especially in preparing circular letters, frame what you have to say so "he who runs may read." This means putting the message in the first lines. When the letter must contain more than a few brief paragraphs, use underlining and paragraph indentation to break up the page and emphasize important things.

A letter may take the place of a call that would involve much more time, and it may be far more effective in the right situation. A pastor's notes have been pivotal at many a turning point in the lives of persons. One minister was surprised to learn that the most distinguished surgeon in his city had one of his notes in a safe-deposit box!

c. The telephone may be a monster or a servant. When the instrument was invented it was used largely for urgent business. Now we are left with the ridiculous convention that a telephone call has the right of way over a personal call and that it should be permitted to break in on anything else, especially if it is from some distance. This is foolish. Morning callers may be told by the secretary or the pastor's wife that he is in the study; " I can call him to the phone, or have him call you at eleven." All but the most importunate will accept the alternative hour, and interruptions of early morning hours will soon stop, except for emergencies.

The telephone may, on the other hand, save hours of driving if you systematically phone families you have already visited at least once, to keep in touch as the years go on. In addition to a routine check of this sort, it is possible to make immediate telephone inquiries when there is any possibility of estrangement, or an apparently casual call when you sense that a member may want to talk about something or ought to do so. Thus the telephone enables one to concentrate personal visits where they are most needed.

d. Office machines, in addition to typewriters, dictating units, and duplicating equipment, may save time and money in larger churches. Addressing machines are available in two major designs. Both have hand-operated and motor-driven models. One relies on small stencils on which the name and address may be typed with an ordinary typewriter. The other uses metal plates. The stencils or plates are easily filed and may be tabbed for special group mailings on the more expensive units. Folding machines, sealing machines, and postage meters have value when there is a large volume of mailing. Most churches will probably be wise to have, instead, a member of the women's association as chairman of bulk mailings. She will receive a schedule well in advance and have teams of women gather at the church for folding, stuffing, sealing, and stamping large mailings.

3. Financial Support

a. Financial support is given to the average church by a little more than two thirds of its communicant membership. Most of these families give a small proportion of income. Those concerned with stewardship will remind members that for their own Christian growth, and out of love for Christ, they should be giving a considerably larger percentage.

b. The group of members concerned with church finances must recommend how the money given is to be used. Some must be forwarded for work of the church beyond the local scene. Most congregations give 15 to 30 percent for this general mission. Many are progressing year by year toward an even division of church income between the local and the world mission, and a few give more for work administered by others. The money retained for local use will be expended to best effect if its detailed use is planned in advance in a budget, and carefully supervised. There should be a monthly comparative report from the treasurer showing in parallel columns: (1) the budget items of income and expense and (2) amounts allocated to each for the year, (3) the actual income and expenditures to the end of the month this year, and (4) comparable figures for the preceding year. These figures are important since income and expenditure for periods of the year will vary on fairly predictable curves and this should be taken into account. Income totals at the end of February may not be two twelfths of the budget in a cold climate, and the whole insurance item may be spent in September. Wise planning will provide that large, single-payment items of expense come at seasons of the year when balances are good. The comparative report will call attention to changes in income which may be significant and will show any tendencies to spend money not available for particular items. Those persons responsible may then take remedial action before this becomes difficult or impossible. The annual financial report of the treasurer may follow the comparative form. It will also list capital funds, showing any changes, and indicating the nature of investments. If there is a different treasurer for benevolent or general mission funds, he may also prepare monthly comparative reports and an annual report.

c. The treasurer will expend money only against items of the budget and will require vouchers from responsible persons except in the case of specific items, such as salaries authorized by actions of the official board. Expenditures outside the budget will require board or congregational action which should include instructions as to a special source of funds or a revision of the budget. An auditor will be appointed or elected each year to examine the treasurer's records, check receipts against deposits, and compare balances in reports with those in banks and investments. This protects the treasurer who will also wish to be bonded if large amounts are involved.

d. Envelopes for weekly offerings are provided by most churches. This makes it easier for members to give on a regular basis, and for the church to keep a record for audit. This system will also be of value to members questioned on credits for income tax reports. Opening envelopes and counting money should be a task for a group, or at least for more than one person. No individual or family should be subjected to the temptation which may seem slight, but has often proved disastrous. Participants may sign an auditor's slip or cash book entry certifying amounts. A record of individual giving may be kept by posting after each member's name in a ruled book the amount written on an envelope by those who opened it. This may be done by the treasurer, a church employee, or a small group. It is essential that information of this sort be held in confidence, so a limited number of workers is desirable. Quarterly statements showing the amount of a member's pledge and the gifts received are mailed by many churches. Some send them only if a contributor has given less than his pledge or has failed to give for more than two weeks. Statements help to avoid mistakes in records, but it must be clear that they are not bills.

e. In the larger churches it is wise to have a simple inventory system that keeps track of supplies needed and on hand. Properly administered, this makes it possible to purchase at favorable prices such things as stationery and paper, disposable plates and napkins, light bulbs, and cleaning supplies.

f. Endowment funds produce continuing income for program. The public announcement of plans for such a fund may result in capital gifts and substantial legacies over a period of years. If the names of those memorialized by gifts to the endowment fund are printed in the calendar at least once a year at Easter or on Memorial Sunday, more and more people may give to this instead of offering physical memorials which are often a source of embarrassment. Investment is a specialized activity. If a congregation has capital funds and does not have at least two members with adequate qualifications and experience, it may be wise to use a denominational holding fund or the investment service of a bank.

4. Housekeeping

Housekeeping has been an essential in the Christian church from the beginning: witness the women who ministered to Jesus and the disciples, and the early election of deacons "to serve tables." (*a*) Communion preparation and the care of utensils and linens must have the attention of a qualified group. (*b*) Flowers add much to services. Someone may find wild flowers or secure floral gifts from gardens, or purchase bouquets from a florist. An annual schedule of donors may be kept, with confirmations and additions each year. Special arrangements may be made for Christmas and Easter and other occasions. Groups may be enlisted for festival decorations. Notices will be prepared concerning memorial flowers. (*c*) Catering arrangements will be made for luncheons and dinners and coffee hours. This may occasionally involve employment of outside helpers or even professional caterers, but usually the work will be done by members. Groups may take responsibility for particular events, or may agree to areas of responsibility for all occasions: the setting up of the dining room, preparation of food in the kitchen, waiting table, dishwashing and cleanup, pouring at coffee hours and teas. (*d*) Cleaning may be left to employed custodians who are usually men, but many churches feel the need of "a woman's touch." A woman may be employed, but groups often take responsibility for keeping the nursery or kitchen or lounge clean and well equipped. Official boards frequently ask women members to supervise the week-to-week cleaning by custodians and to serve with the groups responsible for maintenance.

PART THREE

POWER

CHAPTER XII

Success and Failure

"The secret of success in the ministry," says a cynical proverb, "is to serve a church in a growing community!" One can hardly deny it has a measure of truth if success is to be measured in terms of income and honors and a seat among the mighty of a denomination. Those who are interested in these goals are, however, not found exclusively in burgeoning suburban churches. Some of them have not been able to secure such a place. Others have chosen different goals but have found their idealism hard to maintain. It may not be consistent, but it is certainly human to start out on a journey to the Promised Land and still want the fleshpots of Egypt.

Some pointed thinking about this would probably be good for all of us. There is nothing wrong with a good income and honors and power. One of the glories of our time is that these pleasant things are within reach of a large proportion of the population. Many pastors enjoy them, and there is no reason why they should not, so long as their prosperity does not spell poverty for others. The Creator has placed us in a fruitful world and obviously expects us to enjoy it. His incarnate Son was not an ascetic. He even went so far as to promise that those who sought first the Kingdom of God and its righteousness would have many things added – and he was talking about earthly blessings. It is important to note that these things have nothing to do with success in the ministry. They must be by-products, and they are legitimate in a pastor's life only insofar as they make it possible for him to do his really important work.

1. Criteria of Success

Success for a congregation, and for the pastor who serves it, is to be measured against the divine purposes for the church: worship and mutual nurture and witness. Quantitative norms can, obviously, not be developed for these goals. Since Christ mourned over the multitudes lost without a shepherd, since he went to the cross for all men, since he commanded his followers to make disciples of all peoples, it may be assumed that he is pleased to see large numbers of people respond to his love and take part in the life of his family on earth. But as there is joy in heaven over one sinner who repents, the solitary visit to a humble dwelling may be as important as preaching to thousands. It depends upon one's orders.

The decaying structure in which a handful of young people gather from the streets to play, and occasionally to pray, may be the birthplace of God's new springtime for the earth. The soaring contemporary cathedral, with three services on Sunday morning, may do little more than support dubious secular values. It is equally possible, of course, that the cathedral beautifully serves divine ends, and the crumbling structure houses sterile delusions. The norm for success appears to be not, How much? but, How faithful to God's purposes? This conclusion emphasizes the importance of the planning process in the life of the church.

2. Social Success

It also suggests that social success has importance to the church to the extent that it aids in the performance of God-given tasks. There is a cult of failure in our time, whose devotees are fond of pointing out that all Jesus had to show for a lifetime was a cross. This is simply not so. He had eleven committed men and probably several hundred more. They were shaken by the crucifixion, but ready when his faith was vindicated, to carry his message to the ends of the earth.

Jesus had promised his disciples that they would do greater things than he had done. He had assured them that they would be part of a growing family, despite persecutions. Against appalling odds this came true. The early church enjoyed success.

The writer of the book of The Acts exults in the three thousand souls added to the church on Pentecost. The Christians were thrilled to be taking part in the rapid expansion of their number. The apostle Paul ranged the earth to tell men of Christ and he gave thanks for the prosperity of the churches he founded. It is fashionable in comfortable countries, where the church has a secure place in society, to deplore the recognition of the church by the Empire. The Christians who had struggled and suffered may be pardoned for thinking of it as a victory. If their successors did not always make good use of the hard-bought opportunity, this does not mean that it was not an opportunity.

Social success can be a good thing for the church. It makes possible an enrichment and wide extension of worship, nurture, and witness. It gives more room for theological reflection and social action. Conversely, as Kenneth Latourette has pointed out, social failure may lead to extinction. Christianity's most dangerous foes have sometimes been cultural: " the social or political prestige of a rival religion, the slow weaning away of a rising generation, the ascendancy of a secular system of values, the disappearance of outward cultural observances connected with the faith of the Church, and a rootlessness engendered by an increased mobility of the population." This means that an attempt to baptize culture is in order, for culture shapes men as it is shaped by them. The church has an obligation to bring into captivity to Christ philosophers and writers, politicians and teachers, soldiers and poets, scientists and musicians. The effort is to be made, not to secure a comfortably dominant position for the church; the effort is to be made because these are all men for whom Christ died and because their activities can help or hinder the people of God as they seek, obediently, to include the whole world in the church's life of worship, mutual nurture, and witness.

It does not matter that no minister or church member is a dominant power figure in a community any more than it mattered that Jesus was not. But it does matter whether the whole culture is friendly or hostile to the purposes of the church. Men often assume that this means pastorates among the mighty and wise are the most strategic places. They ignore two facts.

Established people are very resistant to basic changes, or as Jesus put it, "How hardly shall they that have riches enter into the kingdom of God!" The second point they miss is that the shaping of tomorrow is rarely in the hands of those who think they are molding things. It was not Augustus Caesar on his throne, but a village Child who was to be the most influential person of the first century.

3. A Place for Failure?

The story of that Child suggests, furthermore, that there is a place for failure in God's plans. A pastor or a congregation may, by the very fact of their dedication to the divine purposes, be required to face sacrifice and even death. It is certainly plain that martyrdom may, at times, be more effective than cultural dominance, and that suffering servants may be more useful to their Lord than those in prosperity. A downtown church that forms new congregations and gives them leaders and support may lose its preeminent place in a denomination and even die at last to the glory of God. A suburban church that takes a stand on the racial issue at home while it sends colonists to aid an inner-city congregation may have sad statistics, but a good record in heaven. The church that has no dramatic opportunity may never be reported in a colorful article as it quietly pours resources into more exciting places. The pastor who stands by a church in transition, or deliberately accepts a difficult place, may never be known to anyone who seems to matter—but to God.

There is a large place in God's purpose for people like Jeremiah, who died a hated failure in Egypt, and John the Baptist, who was beheaded in prison, and Jesus, who died on his cross. One thinks of James and Stephen and Paul, of Ignatius and Justin Martyr and Cyprian. And only yesterday there was Bonhoeffer. In every case, God's purposes were accomplished through his suffering servants. Despite the worst the world could do, the divine love spread abroad in the earth, God was worshiped, people grew in faith and love, and the witness was heard. Plainly, the church may serve by success or failure. The important thing is faithfulness to God's purposes.

4. Power for the Church

Faithfulness is hard, especially when it must be sustained for a long time in both prosperity and adversity. Where is the power to be found? Jesus Christ gives the church power. He does it by capturing the hearts of men. He loves us, and his love awakens an answering love. He shows us at the heart of the universe, its Creator and Sustainer, one who will go through anything to gather us into a family to live with him in love forever. By word and deed Jesus uses the imagery of the essential human institution, the family, in helping us to understand the nature of Ultimate Reality. The love we see in him relates to the tender bonds of home, then soars beyond. We see in him a love that will stop at nothing and is stopped by nothing, a love that can use even death on a cross and does not hold back from the pain. We see in him a sublime love that offers acceptance of us as though we had attained it. This love of God in Christ has a power to grip our hearts as nothing else can do. In all of life there is nothing stronger than this love. It brings us together at his feet in adoration and mutual concern and it sends us forth to witness.

In addition to this, Jesus Christ gives the church power by making men over. He releases them from the guilt and power of sin, and enables them to live as children of God. This is not merely a theory. The pastor sees it happen. An evil habit falls from a man like a broken chain. Families about to break up are healed. People who hate each other are reconciled. People leave comfortable homes for hard tasks. The power that raised our Lord from the dead is at work in the world. It is the power of Christ who transforms men and gathers them into the church, and gives his body strength. He was right when he said, "I, if I be lifted up from the earth, will draw all men unto me." He was not mistaken when he declared, "I will build my church; and the gates of hell shall not prevail against it."

What gives the church power? The first answer is Jesus Christ. The second answer is the Holy Spirit. Jesus promised, "Ye shall receive power, after that the Holy Ghost is come upon you." Only the Creator Spirit is able to quicken men to new life. Human effort is to no avail without him. Our utter dependence upon God's Spirit is never to be forgotten. All Christians, but ministers in particular, are tempted to exaggerate their part in God's work. It is, after all, the Holy Spirit who brings life to men and gathers them into the divine family through Word and Sacrament. We do not have to be nervous about this. Our part is vital, but instrumental.

In addition to imparting life to each one, the Spirit draws men into fellowship with God and with one another. Without the gift of new life, gatherings of men are no more than crowds or collectives. Without the grace of fellowship, there is no church and the new life is in danger of draining away like streams of water in dry sand. Through the Spirit, people responding to divine love are drawn into communion with God in prayer. This is important to God, for he made us for communion with him, but it is even more important to the church, for without it there is no inflow of power. Most pastors have experienced the difference between a praying church and one where only a few people pray. They know what this means in the preaching and pastoral work and evangelism. Lives are changed and mountains are moved as a result of prayer. Neglect of prayer brings pettiness and stagnation. Happily, there are signs of a widespread renewal of prayer. The Spirit is giving the church power through prayer as he draws us into fellowship with God in Christ.

He also brings us into fellowship with one another. People made over by exposure to the love of God in Christ find themselves caring for one another. They want to be together. They want to help one another. They are consciously part of God's family and develop a family feeling. The effects of this work of the Spirit are found in the worship, mutual nurture, and witness of the church.

Finally, some of the church's power comes from God through believing men. This is the plain implication of Jesus' remark about Peter, "Upon this rock I will build my church." The first stone in the new edifice was a believing man, and the entire structure will be of the same material. Looking over the broken pieces strewn on the ground, one may feel that there is not much to build with, but after each stone is in place one acknowledges a master builder. Peter, the impulsive and wavering man, did not promise much, nor did James and John with their overwhelming inferiority problems, but they turned out to have qualities the church needed. This was true of Polycarp, whose lack of creativity made him an ideal channel for tradition, and of Patrick, who took fourteen years to obtain an education but was just the right man for the crude Ireland of his day. The subsequent flowering of Christian culture inspired by his ministry was far beyond Patrick, but impossible without him. God does not demand of us genius, which is a good thing for most of us, but he does expect hard and effective work, and he is not indifferent to results.

Like Peter, we may be living stones in the church our Lord is building. We have been designed and endowed for the places we occupy. The talents that make us effective are gifts of God. He expects us to use them faithfully. The power he gives the church through men becomes effective as it is focused. It is at this crucial point of fidelity to the divine purposes that the practices of pastoral administration make their contribution, in planning, organization, and the leadership of persons and groups.

Bibliography

Church Administration

Handbook of Church Management, by William H. Leach. Prentice-Hall, Inc., 1958. Encyclopedic, with extensive reference material on program and supporting activities.

Handbook of Church Administration, by Lowell Russell Ditzen. The Macmillan Company, 1962. Emphasis on program and supporting activities, with detailed forms and procedures.

A Ministering Church, by Gaines S. Dobbins. Broadman Press, 1960. Well subtitled "A Guide to the Meaning and Dynamics of the Administrative Process."

Administration Principles and Practices

Professional Management, Theory and Practice, by Theo Haimann. Houghton Mifflin Company, 1962. A historical survey of management, followed by sections on planning, organizing, staffing, directing, and controlling. Bibliography.

Classics in Management, ed. by Harwood F. Merrill. American Management Association, 1960. Fifteen significant quotations, 1825 to 1950.

The Functions of the Executive, by Chester Barnard. Harvard University Press, 1948. A classic.

The Minister's Task

The Church and Its Changing Ministry, ed. by Robert Clyde Johnson. Office of the General Assembly, The United Presbyterian Church in the United States of America, 1961.

The Ministry in Historical Perspectives, ed. by H. Richard Niebuhr and Daniel D. Williams. Harper & Row, Publishers, Inc., 1957.

Preface to Pastoral Theology, by Seward Hiltner. Abingdon Press, 1958.

The Rebirth of Ministry, by James D. Smart. The Westminster Press, 1960.

Minister's Prayer Book, by John W. Doberstein. Fortress Press, 1962.

PLANNING

A Planned Program for the Church Year, by Weldon Crossland. Abingdon Press, 1951.

A Self Study Guide, by the Office of Strategy, Board of National Missions, The United Presbyterian Church U.S.A., 1961. Available in several editions to meet needs of different churches.

How to Get Your Church Built, by C. Harry Atkinson. Doubleday & Company, Inc., 1964. Invaluable guidance in building, altering, or equipping a church.

PERSONNEL

How to Develop Better Leaders, by Malcolm and Hulda Knowles. Association Press, 1957. Clear treatment, with bibliography, film lists, and information on National Training Laboratories.

Developing Competent Subordinates, by James M. Black. American Management Association, 1961. Industrial supervisory practices. See also *Management for Modern Supervisors,* by Carl Heyel (American Management Association, 1962).

The Multiple Staff in the Local Church, by Herman J. Sweet., The Westminster Press, 1963. Wise and thorough.

WORKING WITH GROUPS

Group Leadership and Democratic Action, by Franklyn S. Haimann. Houghton Mifflin Company, 1957. What social scientists have learned about leaders and the dynamics of groups, with ten-page bibliography.

Understanding How Groups Work, Leadership Pamphlet #4.

Adult Education Association, 743 N. Wabash Avenue, Chicago, Ill., 1956. A summary of present knowledge from leaders at University of Michigan, University of Chicago, and University of Illinois. See also *Dynamics of Participative Groups,* by Gibb, Platts, and Miller (University of Colorado Press, 1958), which has bibliography of one hundred books and articles.

Successful Conferences and Discussion Techniques, by Harold P. Zelko. McGraw-Hill Book Company, Inc., 1957.

The Dynamics of Planned Change, by Lippitt, Watson, and Westley. Harcourt, Brace and World, Inc., 1958.

Worship

Christian Worship, by George Hedley. The Macmillan Company, 1953.

Word and Sacrament, by Donald Macleod. Prentice-Hall, Inc., 1960.

Church Music and Theology, by Eric Routley. Fortress Press, 1959. The place of music in the worship of various traditions.

Planning a Year's Pulpit Work, by Andrew W. Blackwood. Abingdon Press, 1942.

Nurture

The Power of God in a Parish Program, by Joseph E. McCabe. The Westminster Press, 1959. Pastoral visitation emphasis.

Pastoral Care in Historical Perspective, by W. Clebsch and C. Jaekle. Prentice-Hall, Inc., 1964.

Protestant Pastoral Counseling, by Wayne E. Oates. The Westminster Press, 1962.

Whom God Hath Joined, by David R. Mace. The Westminster Press, 1953. Superb instruction and counsel for married couples, with daily readings for a month. See also *Love and Conflict,* by Gibson Winter (Doubleday & Company, Inc., 1958), and for the pastor, *The Ethics of Sex,* by Helmut Thielicke (Harper & Row, Publishers, Inc., 1964).

Ye Shall Be Comforted, by William F. Rogers. The Westminster Press, 1950. Help for the sorrowing. This is one of the Westminster Pastoral Aid Books. Others are designed for older people, the sick, the handicapped, the dying, the families of mental patients and alcoholics.

New Life in the Church, by Robert A. Raines. Harper & Row, Publishers, Inc., 1961. Small-group emphasis. See also *Spiritual Renewal Through Personal Groups,* by John L. Casteel (Association Press, 1957).

Religious Education: A Comprehensive Survey, by M. J. Taylor. Abingdon Press, 1960. See also *Facing Adult Problems in Christian Education,* by Helen Khoobyar (The Westminster Press, 1963).

Christian Faith and the Contemporary Arts, ed. by Finley Eversole. Abingdon Press, 1962.

Witness

The Communication of the Christian Faith, by Hendrik Kraemer. The Westminster Press, 1956. Theological analysis. See also the practical *Effective Evangelism,* by George E. Sweazey (Fleming H. Revell Company, 1948).

Where in the World, by Colin W. Williams. National Council of the Churches of Christ in the U.S.A., 1963. Changing forms of the church's witness, and the discussion of the missionary structure of the congregation.

The Mission of the Church in the World, by Louis and André Rétif. Burns Oates & Washbourne, Ltd., London, 1962. Roman Catholics face mass man.

Cities and Churches: Readings on the Urban Church, ed. by Robert Lee. The Westminster Press, 1962. Developments in the urban church, with bibliography. See also *God's Colony in Man's World,* by George W. Webber (Abingdon Press, 1960), and *The Suburban Captivity of the Churches* (Doubleday & Company, Inc., 1961) and *The New Creation as Metropolis* (The Macmillan Company, 1963), both by Gibson Winter.

God's Stewards, by Brattgard. Augsburg Publishing House, 1963. A theological treatment. See also *A Theology for Christian Stewardship,* by T. A. Kantonen (Fortress Press, 1956); *Money and the Church,* by Luther P. Powell (Association Press, 1962), a survey of church support methods; and *Christian Stewardship and Ecumenical Confrontation* (National Council of the Churches of Christ in the U.S.A., 1961), a survey of ecumenical thought.

Telling the Good News, ed. by Johnson, Temme, and Hushaw. Concordia Publishing House, 1962. A comprehensive public relations manual. See also *Public Relations for Your Church,* by Stedman, Rowland, and Heinze (Presbyterian Distribution Center, New York City, 1960), and *Churchmen Let's Go to Press,* by Holt Henderson (Methodist Information, New York City, 1960).

SUPPORTING ACTIVITIES

How to Organize Your Church Office, by Clara A. McCartt. Fleming H. Revell Company, 1962. This is one of Revell's new Better Church Series, which includes booklets on church buildings, staff, libraries, activities, meals, and recruiting teachers.

Index